A Cozy Getaway

A
Cozy Getaway

by Cozy Baker

Illustrations and front cover
designed by Susan Elliot

Published by ACROPOLIS BOOKS LTD. • WASHINGTON, D.C. 20009

Other COZY GETAWAYS in preparation:
Caribbean Getaways
European Getaways
South American Getaways

THE ACROPOLIS TRAVEL AND RECREATION SERIES
Pacific Paradise on a Low Budget
Patternless Fashions
Moku — hanga
New Approaches to Financing
Parks and Recreation
Bicentennial Games in Fun Handbook
Tennis for Everyone
Discover USA
How to Travel the World
and Stay Healthy

© 1976 by Cozy Baker

ACROPOLIS BOOKS LTD.
Colortone Building, 2400 17th St., N.W., Washington, D.C. 20009

Printed in the United States of America by
COLORTONE PRESS Creative Graphics, Inc.
Washington, D.C. 20009

Library of Congress Cataloging in Publication Data

Baker, Cozy, 1927-
  A cozy getaway.

    1. United States--Description and travel--1960-
--Guide-books. 2. Canada--Description and travel--
1951-   --Guide-books. I. Title.
E158.B28   917.3'04'925   76-15816
ISBN 0-87491-063-3

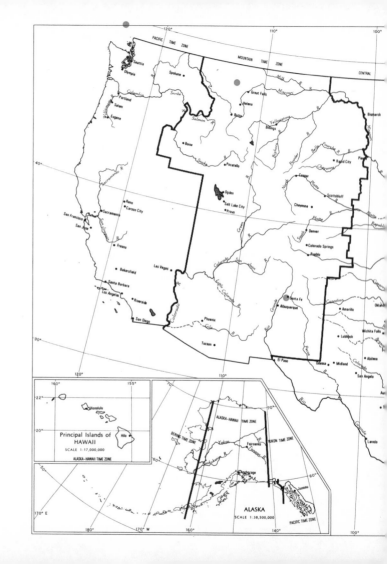

EASTERN TIME ZONE

Albers Equal Area Projection

SCALE 1:17,000,000

| 0 | 100 | 200 | 300 | 400 MILES |

| 0 | 200 | 400 | 600 KILOMETERS |

Standard time zones of the United States
are as of Oct. 1969

Contents

Introduction

More and more travel lovers are looking for alluring out-of-the-way getaways. To these travelers seeking the untouristed, unspoiled and unique *A Cozy Getaway* is dedicated. This personal travel guide specializes in small towns preserving old world charm, larger towns with flavor and flair, places with room to roam, islands to escape from it all, villages with a tang of salt in the air, hideaway retreats and beltway getaways (a special section devoted to places of interest around our Nation's Capital).

In selecting cozy getaways the author kept in mind that some readers would enjoy squeaking snow on a brisk morning while others would prefer cool breezes on a balmy evening. Since personal preferences vary, each getaway is significant either historically, scenically, recreationally, or gastronomically.

Whether you desire to travel or are content to read about the sights and sounds of our beautiful continent, this book takes you to restored 17th century towns, sparkling 20th century cities, isolated islands, fishing villages and a few of the remaining unchanged spectacular vistas of nature. No area of the world offers a more splendid and varied panorama than North America.

Although atmosphere and flavor are stressed, you can find specific inns, restaurants, shops and activities to make your vacation really special. So, pack curiosity and enthusiasm along with your trusty road map. Seek history, beauty, fun and the unexpected in every place you go. Whatever your level of luxury, whatever your time budget, you will find fascinating out-of-the-way getaways for a romantic lunch, an enchanted weekend, or an intriguing sojourn in "A Cozy Getaway."

Small Towns preserving Old World Charm

ABINGDON – A SMALL TOWN WITH BIG IDEAS

TUCKED IN THE EXTREME SOUTHWEST corner of Virginia, just a stone's throw from North Carolina and Tennessee, Abingdon is a different kind of town. I saw a reflection of Abingdon's special difference in the eyes of a young lady as she talked about "my town." Leah's eyes literally glowed as she described the people and charms of this small quiet town in the foothills of Virginia's Blue Ridge Mountains.

Its original brick sidewalks and century-old brick homes attest to the fact that Abingdon is the oldest town in southwest Virginia. Abingdon is the name of Martha Washington's ancestral home and is the county seat of America's first county to be named for George Washington.

It was the simple idea of bartering food for theater tickets, however, that put Abingdon on the map. The Barter Theater was born in 1932 when a hungry actor conceived the idea of exchanging underfed talent for an overabundance of produce. The challenge of taking theater into remote places was almost as invigorating as the possibility of exchanging ham for Hamlet.

Robert Porterfield, a native Virginian, worked as an actor in New York during the Depression. Scarcity of work gave him plenty of time to think. He was struck by the irony of New York's plethora of jobless actors and his hometown's abundance of unsold crops. Uniting these two concepts was a major undertaking which resulted in the South's largest and oldest theater.

America's first state subsidized theater has launched many notable actors

10

on a spiraling career while offering the people of Virginia an opportunity to observe and perform in some of the world's most distinguished productions. Gregory Peck and Ernest Borgnine are two who began here.

Barter's season extends from June to October with a varied bi-weekly program. Even if you see Miss Mary arriving with a fresh chicken or a bouquet of flowers, it would behoove you to have a little cash in your pocket. The theater now operates on a cash basis although it makes exceptions for some old timers.

Martha Washington Inn, across the street from the theater, is as integral a part of Abingdon as The Barter Theater. The Inn has been associated with the town's historical, cultural, educational and social life since 1830. It was built as a private residence and later became a college. At present the Inn's one hundred rooms are individually decorated and furnished with genuine antiques.

Spacious verandahs with rocking chairs and a graceful winding stairway are as much an Abingdon institution as the Inn's good old Southern cooking. Country ham, spoon bread, pecan muffins and hot biscuits are a few of their popular dishes. Hooray for that Southern hospitality!

Abingdon's rural small town pace accelerates to a crescendo the first two weeks of August during the annual Virginia Highlands Festival. Activities include sidewalk art shows, a flea market, an antique car show, candlelight tours of old homes and a continuous antique show. Musical programs range from strolling minstrels to jazz concerts. Square dancing, ballet, and modern dance performances are held also. It's possible to go backstage at the Barter Theater and dine with the actors at the Inn.

All-day craft demonstrations are conducted in spinning, weaving, pottery, wood carving, rug hooking, broom making, chair caning, basket weaving and you name it. I don't believe you could come up with a folk art that isn't represented. Why you can even learn to make honeysuckle baskets and Raggedy Ann, clothes

11

pin, corn shuck and apple face dolls.

In addition to the craft demonstrations there are numerous seminars open to the public. They include classes in drama, music, art, photography and creative writing.

The Martha Washington Inn with its spacious rooms and lawn is headquarters for many of these colorful events. The whole town joins in this exciting festival and each year new entries are added to an already bulging schedule.

Actually, there is more to Abingdon than a theater and an Inn. The Cave House Craft Shop on Main Street, named for the Victorian structure which houses the shop, claims that Daniel Boone tied up his dogs where the Cave House now stands and went across the street to what was to become the famous Wilderness Road. The craft shop is operated by a non-profit marketing cooperative serving local crafts people. If the festival demonstrations haven't convinced you that you can do it yourself, here's your chance to buy a unique, handmade gift. And if you don't find what you are looking for, they will make it.

Cumbow China Decorating Company on the same street features world-famous hand-decorated china. At Iron Mountain Stoneware in Laurel Bloomey, Tennessee (about 15 miles from Abingdon), they make beautiful, serviceable dishes, place settings, etc. So, if you need some pretty new breakfast dishes or a handsome wedding gift, you might drive across the state border.

The hundred mile drive from Abington to Roaring Gap along Routes 58 and 21 is sheer mountain *beautery*. Closer by White Top Mountain and Mother State Park are two scenic excursions you'll enjoy. South Holston Dam and Lake, just five miles South of Abingdon provides good boating, fishing and water skiing. And for an authentic touch of old world, drive out Whites Mill Road. The old water wheel of Whites Mill still turns to grind corn meal just right for hush puppies and hoe cake.

That brings me back to my friend whose eyes told me about Abingdon. After my visit she dropped me a note in which she wrote, "The country side encompassing Abingdon is as beautiful as I will ever see, pasture-land, farmland, mountainous terrain—friendly country people. If you do mention Abingdon, please don't slight it." Thank you, Leah Fleenor. I discovered Abingdon is indeed special.

GREENFIELD VILLAGE–PORTRAIT OF THE PAST

AMERICAN HISTORY IS ALIVE at Greenfield Village. Within sight, but not sound, of Detroit's bustling beltway is a quiet, picturesque village depicting Americana as it existed for three and a half centuries.

Greenfield is no ordinary restored village. Instead, over a hundred original buildings from across the nation were disassembled, shipped and reassembled as a town in the heart of Dearborn, Michigan. Dearborn is the birthplace of Henry Ford whose objective was to construct an accurate replica of American life as it existed prior to 1900. This couldn't have been accomplished with more tasteful authenticity.

Greenfield Village is an unparalleled outdoor museum paying tribute to the dramatic growth of America's inventive genius from home crafts to industry. Sheep graze in the shadows of a Cape Cod windmill. Craftsmen work at skills you seldom see today; shodding horses, cutting and stitching leather beer mugs and taking tin-type photos.

The Village Green is complete with church, courthouse, town hall, schools and Inn. Radiating from this focal point are the homes and workshops of America's great inventors as well as typical 17th, 18th and 19th century houses and craft shops. In some cases the very soil under the building was moved here.

In tracing the development of American life, Greenfield Village has brought Costwold Cottage and Forge from England. The unique rose cottage with walled garden, barnyard and dovecote illustrates a typical homestead of our English forefathers.

Edison's first laboratory, the Wright Brothers cycle shop, Noah Webster's house and Abraham Lincoln's courthouse are all here. Many of the buildings have costumed guides, others tell a story with the push of a button.

You can ride around the Village in a real steam train, travel its quaint streets in a Model-T or carriage and take a ride on a paddle-wheel steamboat or a 1913 merry-go-round.

To insure the pervasive leisurely pace, children under 15 must be accompanied by an adult. No carnival attractions, neon lights or hot dog stands. Yet there is enchantment for all ages. Turn-of-the-century family entertainment includes a half-hour musical revue at the Town Hall. A typical medicine man act on the Village Green keeps them laughing on the lawn.

Snacks and sumptuous meals are served in attractive restaurants throughout the complex. Upstairs at Heritage Hall you can dine in colonial candlelit elegance. Or enjoy an open-hearth grill at the Riverfront Restaurant, to mention a few.

Each season has its own charm. Various special events are staged throughout the year. They include a Country Fair of Yesteryear, an Old Car Festival, a Muzzle Loaders Festival, a Colonial Military Muster and an Autumn Harvest Weekend.

The adjacent Ford Museum is immense. At the entrance a beautiful staircase leads to Ford's personal collection, including over 3000 clocks and timepieces. Transportation is remarkably exhibited with a collection of 200 automobiles, full-sized steam locomotives, airplanes, boats, carriages and bicycles. The entire course of the Industrial Revolution from pre-steam power days to the jet age is traced with a comprehensive assemblage of tools and machines.

A "Street of Early American Shops" affords an amazing glimpse into the past through replicas of craft shops and stores stocked with appropriate period collections. Decorative art galleries present a treasure of furniture, glass, silver and textiles used from the Pilgrim period through the 19th century.

These in-depth exhibits indoors combined with the extensive outdoor settings constitute an unmatched museum complex.

Dearborn offers more for vacationers than Greenfield Village and the Ford Museum. Many parks and wooded areas along the banks of the Rouge River are perfect for picnics. For the golfer, Dearborn Hills is a beautifully challenging course. Children are delighted with the zoo, Indian exhibits at the old Arsenal Building, the Parlor, featuring old fashioned frozen custard, and Dearborn's Youth Center.

Henry Ford's "Scottish Baronial" Mansions with 56 rooms, 15 baths and a bowling alley is open to the public. Fairlane Mansions, named for Ford's ancestral home in northern Ireland, is surrounded by gardens, winding paths and woodlands.

In addition to housing 200,000 volumes, Henry Ford's library is the setting for a magnificent Memorial fountain and reflection pool. One of the multi-jet sprays shoots more than 40 feet into the blue. A spiral staircase or elevator will take you to the third floor where you can listen from a collection of 10,000 stereo and regular records.

Museums galore, from Ford's Rouge Plant to Dearborn's Institute of Art, theater, concerts, shops and good restaurants—whatever it takes to make your getaway pleasant, you'll probably find in Dearborn. Many good motels and hotels are available. Just a couple of blocks from Greenfield Village is a gem—Dearborn Inn. Huge elms shade the stately Motor House and five colonial homes. These luxurious accommodations capture the atmosphere of gracious hospitality as it was appreciated years ago. Swimming pools, tennis courts, delicious food and many homey touches make this an ideal headquarters for your visit to a quieter century.

COOPERSTOWN –REFLECTIONS OF YORE ON GLIMMERGLASS

ALONG THE QUIET SHORES of a glimmering lake, Cooperstown remains a "provincial town of importance." James Fenimore Cooper unwittingly used this term to describe the village founded by his father in 1786. Referring to Lake Otsego as "Glimmerglass," Cooper used this wilderness setting for two of his famous novels, *The Deerslayer* and *The Pioneers.*

Located in central New York, seventy miles West of Albany, Cooperstown is a charming, colorful, calm resort town. Baskets of flowers hang from every lamp post. Victorian homes and stately inns on wide, tree-shaded streets enhance an old-fashioned ambience that permeates the air.

The drive from Albany passes through scenic Schoharie and Cherry Valleys. Quaint villages with white frame houses and tapered church spires dot the wooded hillsides. Nine miles from Cooperstown you spy Otsego Lake through the trees. Soon it comes into full view, following the country road into town.

The Farmers' Museum and Village Crossroads portray rural life in New York between 1783 and 1840. Picturesque buildings sprawl over hundreds of acres of lush rolling farmland. In a recreated 19th century village you can observe craftsmen working at trades that were indispensable to everyday life. Moved here with loving care, some of the buildings serve the same functions today as they did when first constructed.

You will see a one-room schoolhouse, doctors' and lawyers' offices and a druggist shop. At the country store you can buy licorice and rock candy. Approaching Lippitt Homestead you may catch a whiff of freshly baked bread—maybe Sally Lunn. The printing office and blacksmith shop are still active. It's fun to watch lambs, chickens, cows and even oxen roaming around the village grounds. Bump Tavern and the Homestead barn typically portray the era and a graceful country church completes this tranquil town of yore.

Across the road from the Farmer's Museum stands an elegant ivy-covered stone mansion. Build in 1932 on the site of a cottage once occupied by the Coopers, Fenimore House is the home of the New York State Historical Association. It contains an outstanding collection of American Folk Art. Paintings, wood carvings, metal work, needlework and scrimshaw exemplify the roots of rural crafts in the period from 1783 to 1840. One room is devoted to Cooper memorabilia. In another, life masks of early American presidents and leaders of the Republic are cast in bronze by J. H. I. Browen. A bookshop near the entrance has an excellent selection of volumes pertaining to the area.

On a velvet landscaped lawn sloping to the lakeside, the Otesaga Hotel, girded with towering white columns and topped by an imposing cupola, epitomizes gracious hospitality as it existed a century ago. Its spacious public rooms, luxurious bedrooms, hearth-warmed lounges and verandahs overlooking the lake are geared to your comfort.

The hotel complex includes a beautiful 18-hole championship golf course that skirts the lakefront on either side. A heated swimming pool, shuffleboard areas, tennis courts, a putting green, water skiing and sailing facilities, add up to a country-estate resort that is hard to beat.

On a smaller scale and older note, the Cooper Inn exemplifies leisurely luxury. Located in the heart of the village, this quiet inn has been welcoming visitors since 1812. Its rooms are a treasure house of antiques. Suites are available as well as a few individual cottages.

If you are a baseball fan, you already know that Cooperstown is the home of the National Baseball Hall of Fame. But do you know why? Well, Abner Doubleday is said to have invented our national pastime in Cooperstown in 1839. So, one hundred years later a museum and hall of fame were launched to honor the great American game and its players. It depicts the growth and development of the sport with plaques of the greats and countless mementos like gloves, bats and balls, all worn, swung and thrown by baseball heroes. Major league buffs and little leaguers alike will revel in this collection which includes Babe Ruth's locker.

Being an ardent fancier of Cinderella's coach and Quebec's calèche (in fact, any horse and buggy), I found The Carriage and Harness Museum a rare treat. This unusual assemblage of custom-made carriages is the private collection of one man. From a pony runabout to a handsome road coach, you'll find every type of horse-drawn sports vehicle. Housed in the owner's original stables, these carriages have been carefully preserved. With a push of a button you can hear various coach horn calls.

If it's the call of the wild that beckons you, you'll be delighted with the Indian Museum and Busch Woodlands Museum. Combining nature with history, you can stroll through the woods and see exhibits of Indian artifacts and dioramas depicting novels by James Fenimore Cooper. Ride on an old horse-drawn street car or take a 16-mile "cross-country" jaunt on the Cooperstown and Charlotte Valley steam locomotive. Authentic old passenger cars are complete with dining car service.

These attractions are fun but the real appeal of Cooperstown for me is its relaxed atmosphere. This attractive town reflected in deep blue waters retains a serenity not easy to find in these hectic, hurried days.

In prophesizing the future of Cooperstown in 1838, Cooper further stated that the "beauty of its situation, the lake, the purity of the air and the other advantages already pointed out, seem destined to make it more peculiarly a place of resort, for those who live less for active life than for its elegance and ease." That description sums up what Cooperstown is all about.

ECHOING A STYLE AND TEMPO of more leisurely days, Old Salem, in the heart of Winston-Salem, retains the true spirit of an 18th century town. Salem, the Hebrew word for peace, was built in North Carolina's wilderness by stout-hearted Moravian Brethren in 1766. These devout Germanic people believed in a close-knit family life, a strong work ethic and had an abiding faith in God. This quiet, peaceful town has been designated a National Historic Landmark. Many of its restored buildings are private residences that enhance the authentic atmosphere of this living museum.

Even among early American towns, Salem was an unusual community. It was a "congregation town" where all residents lived pretty much as one big family. Earthly as well as spiritual matters were under the direction of the church.

Home Moravian Church, built in 1800, has retained many of its rich traditions while maintaining a broad purposeful program for its active 20th century congregation. Music is almost as vital to the Moravian religion as prayer. Mellow tones from a 1797 organ, voices of a children's choir or beats of a spirited band may reverberate from the large church on Salem Square at any time. Love feasts are a meaningful tradition still cherished. Celebrating occasions of deep spiritual significance, the congregation shares sweet rolls and coffee in the light of hand-made beeswax candles to the refrain of the Moravian Song of the Morning Star. The whole town joins in this cherished ceremony at Easter time and Christmas Eve.

Majestic laurel oaks line a path leading into God's Acre, the Moravian Burial Ground. Rows of identical flat, white gravestones symbolize their precept of democracy in death. Graves may not be distinguished between rich and poor, but burial is according to "choirs" (married men, single women, age, etc.) rather than by families.

The Moravians followed a democratic tenet in their daily lives also. One of the major buildings open to the public is Single Brothers House. Boys came here at the age of 14 to learn a craft. Doing their own housekeeping, single men continued to live together.

You don't have to ask which building is Winkler Bakery. The smell of freshly baked bread and ginger cookies directs you to this quaint restored bakery where you can watch the baker and his assistants molding loaves in the front room, then placing them in a wood-fired oven in the back room.

No cheap concessions or souvenir stands mar the quiet, shaded streets. But you can buy some lovely pewter and china items at the Old Salem Store and some fine antiques next door. Between these two shops is the dearest little garden. Four wisteria vine trees completely canopy a tiny brick courtyard. A few small benches are secluded among ivy and ferns. I overheard one girl exclaiming that this was exactly the enchanted garden she wanted for her wedding.

The Boys School houses the Wachovia Museum which includes a special exhibit (with sound) of Moravian musical instruments and manuscripts.

A weatherboarded log house, built in 1771, is the oldest tobacco shop in America. You can also see the market-fire house with two fire engines which were first demonstrated in 1785.

The Salem Tavern plays a dual role. One building (the first brick structure in Salem) houses a museum and the other contains dining rooms where luncheon and dinner are served by costumed waiters. Menu specialties include numerous German dishes and many local people think the Tavern has the best food in town. Weather permitting, you can enjoy lunch on a delightful, wisteria-arbored terrace. Inside, four of the six dining rooms have fireplaces and the decor is early 19th century style.

Rooms are no longer available for overnight lodging, but a few miles from town you can find accommodations at Tanglewood. This special hotel is a complete recreational resort in a sylvan setting of serenity. Accommodations range from rustic cottages in the woods and modern motel rooms to luxurious suites with double canopied beds and fireplaces in a gracious old Manor House.

Delicious meals in the tradition of the old South are served in five Colonial dining rooms. Beautiful terraces and gardens surround the old homeplace. Roads wind through a secluded woodland park which contains two 18-hole championship golf courses, with two lavish club houses, a par-3 course, driving range, miniature golf, tennis courts, olympic pool, children's play areas and camping grounds. There are horses for riding, paddleboats and canoes for boating on two sparkling lakes, and a barn that has been converted into a summer theater. Casual elegance and an easy relaxed tempo are the keynotes to Tanglewood. Make reservations well in advance. (Address: Tanglewood, Clemmons, North Carolina 27012, phone: 919–766-6461.)

More early 20th century elegance is in evidence at Reynolda House, the former home of R. J. Reynolds. Here, in palatial surroundings, you can view American paintings dating from 1755 to the present. The mansion was the heart of a 1000 acre private village in 1917. Most of the original buildings are still standing. Some have been converted into shops. Exquisite gardens encircling the estate are beautifully maintained and music, drama and art festivals are part of an extensive cultural program at Reynolda House.

On a different note, the R. J. Reynolds Tobacco Company conducts personalized tours through one of the world's most modern and attractive cigarette plants. You can also take a free tour of the Schlitz Brewing Company and enjoy the hospitality of their "Brown Bottle" room.

Be sure to drive through the beautiful campuses of Wake Forest and nearby Graylyn. Sunday concerts at sunset by the Winston-Salem Symphony make Graylyn's palatial lawns a delightful summer rendezvous.

Of all the peaceful, restful parks you'll find, it's historic Bethabara, site of the first Moravian settlement in North Carolina. Even the air feels fresher in this quiet oasis. A church built in 1788, a 1756 palisade fort, a hilltop God's Acre and foundation walls and cellars of recently unearthed buildings are scattered throughout Bethabara.

Somehow the spirit of the Moravians—their zeal for education, work with their hands, their love of music and their faith in God,—has been rekindled. Music, art and education permeate the entire city. Winston-Salem reveres its rich heritage while breathing the spirit of today.

SARATOGA–LORE OF THE PAST AND LURE OF THE PRESENT

SARATOGA'S RICH HERITAGE is steeped in historic battles, mineral waters, horse racing, great hotels, famous homes, entertainment and beautiful people. Its lure today includes the performing arts and other attractions, especially beautiful people.

Ensconced in the foothills of New York's Adirondack Mountains, Saratoga Springs fluctuated from a crude frontier village to a flamboyant resort area, experienced a decline in popularity and emerged to its present status of "historical town makes good"–(real good).

The people of Saratoga are just great. They take immense pride in their scenic and historic town. It is through their loyal support and financial contributions that the city is re-emerging into a year-round vacationer's delight.

Mineral waters brought the pioneers, founders and believers to Saratoga. Ranked among the finest in the world, these waters have a natural carbonation. Baths in the bubbly mineralized waters are a medically proven relief for arthritis, rheumatism and circulatory disorders and a luxurious remedy for tension, nerves and fatigue. For this reason, New York State built a $4 million dollar spa complex in the early 1930's.

Open year round, this is an ideal and inexpensive way to feel relaxed, refreshed and revitalized. A treatment includes twenty minutes in a tub of body temperature carbonated water, a twenty minute massage by a licensed masseur or masseuse, after which you are wrapped in hot sheets and left to relax or sleep in a private bed. This Saratoga experience can be yours for as little as $5.25 during the off season.

Not only are the minerals beneficial to the body, many enjoy the taste. Six springs within the city are free to the public. (Take a glass with you.)

At the height of Saratoga's brilliant social era when the gambling casino was queen of entertainment and characters like Diamond Jim and Lillian Russell adorned the scene, the town boasted the country's largest hotels and sensational Victorian mansions.

The opulent Casino is now a museum. Rooms highlighting Saratoga's unique past are located in the upper floors which originally housed the highstake gambling rooms. The first floor ballroom and grand parlor are open to the public for social and civic events.

Devotees of Mid-Victorian splendor will be delighted with Saratoga's diversified styles of mid-19th century architecture. The Batcheller House is a perfect example. Its many gables are climaxed by a spiring minaret-capped tower. Tour maps with notes on history and architectural styles are available at the Chamber of Commerce, 297 Broadway.

Stateley old Gideon Putnam in its park-like setting still offers all the advantages of a resort. A large modern Holiday Inn with landscaped courtyard and pool is convenient to the Spa facilities. Each of its attractive rooms overlooks Congress Park, containing 20 beautifully landscaped acres. The Italian Gardens in this mid-town park were designed by Henry Bacon, architect of Lincoln Memorial in Washington, D.C. And it was Daniel C. French, noted for the sculpture of the seated Lincoln there, who sculpted the garden's Spirit of Life Fountain.

Saratoga Race Course, the nation's oldest thoroughbred track, comes alive in August with the influx of racing fans from all over the globe. If harness racing appeals to you plan to visit in the Spring. The season runs from mid-April until mid-May on the most beautiful one-half mile track in the country.

Whether you are a racing enthusiast or not, you'll enjoy the National Museum of Racing. It contains one of the world's greatest collections of equine art and racing mementos and houses the Hall of Fame for jockeys, trainers and horses.

Three culinary "institutions" are said to have originated in Saratoga—pie a la mode, the club sandwich and potato chips. The chip story is amusing. Back in 1853 an irate chef at Moon Tavern, disgusted with a customer's continued complaint that his fried potatoes were cut too thick, sliced them paper thin, threw them in hot grease and created instant potato chips! Instead of being annoyed, the diner ate them with relish and the Tavern's reputation for great potatoes became widespread.

Of newer origin, Saratoga's Performing Arts Center is home for the New York City Ballet during July and the Philadelphia Orchestra during August. Guest artists are scheduled from June to September. Rock or Rachmanioff— you'll find it all in their beautiful amphitheater, seating 5000 with lawnspace for 10,000 more.

Saratoga's National Historic Park commemorates the decisive victory in 1777 that marked the turning point of the American Revolution. On this battlefield the American troops defeated the English Army of General John Burgoyne at the Battle of Saratoga. With the surrender of the British Army the constant struggle for control of the Hudson Valley ceased. Saratoga is truly significant in American history.

You can watch a colorful film explaining the battle and follow the battle action over a network of roads. An unusual granite monument is bound to catch your attention. "Monument to a Leg" is at the site of a charge that is credited with deciding the battle. It depicts the left boot and epaulets of the American officer who led the charge in spite of a serious leg wound. Benedict Arnold's name is omitted. But the inscription commemorates "one of the most brilliant soldiers of the Continental Army."

Other parks around Saratoga provide a variety of pleasures. Many fine golf courses are open to the public. Saratoga Lake, nearby Sacandaga Lake and Lake George offer good boating, fishing and swimming. Amusement parks galore for the young set. Petrified Gardens feature an unusual reef of ancient petrified plants, an outdoor museum of sundials, a lily pond and a deer park.

For holidays that join today's recreations with the tempo and grandeur of an era past, plan to spend a few days in Saratoga Springs.

Larger Towns with Flavor and Flair

FROM ITS GLITTERING GREEN rooftops, through intriguing narrow streets of age-old buildings, to the city's verandah, the St. Lawrence River, Quebec City is joie de vivre! Quebec, when mentioned, evokes the same joyous smiles and knowing nods of pleasure as does another queen city, San Francisco. Tempting as it is to compare Quebec's various charms to the best in other cities, Dickens wrote, "It is a place not to be forgotten or mixed up in the mind with other places. . . ."

Perched high atop sheer cliffs above the river, Quebec is the only walled city in North America. Champlain (Father of New France) founded this natural bastion in 1608. The British scaled its heights and took Quebec in 1759. Very little changes occurred under British rule, however. Quebec remains fascinatingly French: language, food, and atmosphere.

Old Quebec is built on two levels. Resembling a medieval castle, Chateau Frontenac crowns the upper promontory. Its turrets and towers are visible from land, sea and air. Although there are modern hotels and quaint pensions to choose from, the Frontenac is a superb choice. It is the focal point for everything.

From Place d'Armes in front of the hotel tours originate—bus, taxi, calèche (horsedrawn carriage) or walking. I suggest the carriage ride to get an overall picture, then several walking excursions. This is the best way to feel the true character of Canada's oldest, most picturesque city.

You will see Dufferen Terrace, a remarkable wooden promenade extending from the Frontenac to the star-shaped citadel. Plains of Abraham, now called Battlefield Park, is just that: a large, grassy, beautiful park, once a battlefield, now a place of "quiet, rest and peace." As you pass along Grande-Allee, one of the principal thoroughfares, you will be charmed by its diverse architecture—gabled and mansarded parliament buildings, cathedral spires, handsome old houses and massive arches penetrating the city's stone walls. Monuments abound. One in Jardin des Gouverneurs uniquely honors two opposing generals and is inscribed: "Valour gave them a common death, history a common fame, posterity a common monument."

Lower Town, reached by cable car or an iron staircase, is the oldest section of Quebec. No traffic is allowed on narrow winding streets where historic stone buildings have been converted into unique shops, restaurants and museums. The entire area is being restored.

Place Royale, the center square, is the site of the Notre-Dame-des-Victories Church. Built in 1688, it has also served as a fort, a residence and a trading post. Of particular interest is a model sailing vessel hanging from the ceiling.

L'Eperlan is a delightful new restaurant located in an old residence. Pleasing decor, excellent seafood and martinis second to none. La Trait du Roi is another interesting restaurant in the Lower Town. From the nearby docks, ferries leave for Levis every 30 minutes. The ride takes 15 minutes and if you stay on the boat a round-trip costs only 50¢. This is a splendid way to view the city, especially at sunset, and undoubtedly the best bargain in town.

Strolling is a favorite pastime of Quebekers as well as tourists. Some streets feature outdoor art galleries, others are lined with smart shops and restaurants. In fact, nearly every block has a half-dozen attractive eating places. La Poudriere is built right into the massive walls of the St. Louis Gates. Aux Anciens Canadiens, a cozy dining spot in one of the oldest houses in Quebec, and the Continental, a classic French restaurant, are all located on St. Louis Street.

Le Vendome, between Upper and Lower Town on La Cote de la Montagne, has authentic accents of Paris and excellent meals at a reasonable price. Two doors away at Jean Alart's Sous le Cap I bought a gorgeous hand-woven ankle length cape with hood. It was just right for the Quebec Winter Carnival.

Pictures of this once-upon-a-time city wrapped in ermine convinced me to wend my way North the two weeks preceding Lent. During this time the entire city is transformed into a crystal palace. Dufferen Terrace is converted into a giant toboggan slide ending right in front of the Frontenac. Heavy lap robes cover bundled passengers in the cocheres. Hearts are as warm in Quebec during snowtime as summertime.

In the shadows of Quebec lies a small island, the Isle D'Orleans, which retains the simplicity of rural life as it existed three centuries ago. Hardly any modern buildings have been constructed. In fact, construction of any kind is virtually at a standstill. Exuding a flavor strongly old-world French, its tranquil countryside was used to portray French scenes in the 1946 film "13 rue Madeleine."

A bridge 12 miles North of the city leads to the timeless island. A paved road, following the river, winds through the six parishes of Isle d'Orleans. The view of Quebec from the island is spectacular. The horizon rimmed with a dazzling skyline of progress contrasts sharply with the island's tiny chapels by the sea, apple orchards sloping to the shores, cattle grazing in verdant fields and brightly gardened farmhouses.

Roadside stands are ablaze with strawberries (one of the island's claims to fame), apples, plums, blueberries and vegetables during summer months. This fresh produce, along with local handicrafts lures shoppers from the mainland.

Many of the original stone churches and farmhouses built in the mid-1600's are still in use. A few have been converted into restaurants. At L'Atre a horse-drawn buggy carries you from the car to a 17th-century house. Meals cooked in front of you on a large stone hearth are enhanced by costumed waitresses and 17th-century chamber music.

Les Ancêtres is an intimate little spot where no English is spoken and you are served whatever is cooking (sans menu). "Le Domaine du Seigneur Mauvide," an old manor house built in 1734, is a museum where you can buy antiques and art crafts. In its peasant-type restaurant they serve popular local items like hot slices of bread covered with thick cream and maple sugar.

Originally a flour mill, "Le Moulin de Saint-Laurent" is situated beside a waterfall that formerly drove the wheel. Typically French, the walls and floors are chinked stone and copper kettles hang from heavy-beamed rafters. Musicians add to the romantic atmosphere during dinner. A European menu includes Dutch hors-d'oeuvres, Viennese veal-cutlets, French crepes and Hungarian goulash with a choice of German and Roumanian wines.

Hotels and guest houses are few and far between (verging on the nonexistent). Belluevue Hotel at Sainte-Petronille is open July and August. Its rambling verandah has an uninterrupted view of Quebec City and the maritime traffic navigating the St. Lawrence waterway. It was from St. Petronille that General Wolfe bombarded Quebec in 1759.

The Beaupre coastline with towering steeples etched against the Laurentian Mountains comes into view at the Northern end of the island. Sainte-Anne-de-Beaupre has been one of America's most famous shrines since the mid-17th century. Inside the Romanesque Basilica stacks of crutches and braces attest to the healing cures acclaimed by many.

35

"Cyclorama," the world's largest painting, is located at St. Anne D'Beaupre. A 360-foot circular panorama creates a three-dimensional illusion of life in the Holy Land on the day of crucifixion. From an observation platform you hear a narrator explaining the scenes of historical and religious significance. The masterpiece completed by a team of fine artists has been inspiring viewers since 1895.

Great tranquility permeates nearby Scala Santa Chapel. Crowds don't linger in this simple chapel, but I was touched by three penitents kneeling their way up steep steps of atonement.

Equally inspiring was an outdoor hillside Way of the Cross. Bronze, life-size figures depicting Christ's last days of passion and death on the cross are postured at intervals along sylvan paths. Pilgrims are led in prayer by monks as they move from station to station.

Returning to Quebec, you get a fabulous view of Montmorency Falls. Looming dramatically by the side of the road, the falls are 274 feet high, one and a half times higher than Niagara. The thundering cascades are mystically impressive, especially when winter's icy winds crystallize the spray mist into one massive cone.

There is no doubt about it, whatever the season, Quebec City and its surrounding countryside is Joie de Vivre.

THE IDEA OF AN IDYLLIC resort conjures mental images of open roads and rolling countryside, but it isn't necessarily so. **Cross Keys Inn** in the city of Baltimore has all the essentials for a luxurious mini-vacation. (Directions: I-95 to Exit 26 (I-695). Turn West to Exit 23; follow Route 83S to Northern Parkway Exit; turn left to Falls Rd., then right to Cross Keys Village.)

Right in the midst of Cross Keys Village, a distinctive community of private residences, businesses and shops, you will find Cross Keys Inn. Its modernistically decorated rooms are spacious. Some have steam baths, bars and a view of the engaging village green.

Landscaped and encircled by attractive botiques and shops, the green is perfect for strolling, shopping or enjoying a snack at the trellised sidewalk cafe. Instead of an expensive meal, you might select your favorite goodies at the nearby delicatessen and brown bag it to the al fresco tables.

Among the array of shops you will find an exclusive dress shop, book store, art gallery and ice cream parlor. One store features magnificent hand-made wooden furniture, a flower shop has an extensive selection of rare plants and several gift shops sell everything from hibachis to hammocks.

Swimming and indoor tennis are available for the sports enthusiasts. A superb restaurant and a handsome lounge with nightly entertainment complete a perfect setup for a perfect weekend getaway.

# # #

Taking Exit 24 off 695, you approach **Hunt Valley Inn** and Golf Club. Spawling at the foot of Maryland hills, this elegant but casual resort caters to your every whim. For the non-golfer there is tennis, bicycle and horseback riding and skeet shooting.

Tucked off the main lobby are the Rendezvous Lounge and Paddock Bar and Cinnamon Tree Restaurant. This elegant dining room derives its name from the spectacular bronze and copper sculptured tree dominating the gold and brown scene. Fortunately the cuisine proves as excellent as the decor, so all appetites can be satisfied.

Decorators have spared no details in the lavishly appointed rooms and suites. The whole idea of the Hunt Valley Inn—to surround you with beauty and comfort in a gracious Maryland manner—has been accomplished.

# # #

If your time budget is geared closer to an afternoon than a weekend, then how's about **Haussner's**? For a lunch that combines an art exhibit and museum tour with a savory meal and good drinks you can't beat Haussner's.

Originally a salesman's lunch counter in the East section of Baltimore, this unbelievable establishment has grown to encompass five row houses. Each is chock full of art treasures collected by Mrs. Haussner from all over the world. Literally a thousand paintings, including some by Rembrandt, Homer and Whistler, cover the walls frame to frame. Every nook and cranny is filled with antique furnishings and fine bronze and marble sculptures. Corner cabinets are filled with exotic curios. Christmas plates, Bavarian plates and plates of every type rim the molding around the high ceiling.

Although the menu is almost as extensive as the art collection, Stephen George, the manager, insists Haussner's food is basic rather than gourmet. In lieu of a chef, there is a kitchen manager and everyone in the kitchen, including the waitresses, share equal billing.

The entire staff joins in reflecting Haussner's premise that the public deserves fine food, fine service and fine art. Many customers have been returning for this happy combination since the 30's. Many of the original waitresses are still on the scene.

Do not let the policy of no advertising, no reservations, no parking and no credit cards deter you. Whether you are in the mood for German food, seafood or fancy Austrian pastries, you will enjoy a trip to Haussner's. (Directions: I-95 to 695 through Harbor Tunnel to O'Donnel Street exit; west to Clinton Street; turn right to 3244 Eastern Avenue—Closed Sunday and Monday.)

# # #

Another Baltimore restaurant which does not advertise or take reservations is **Maison Marconi** (106 W. Saratoga St.). Residents of Baltimore have been spreading the raves by word of mouth for years. Continental cuisine is served in the rather formal dining room of an old townhouse. An interesting innovation is that drinks are mixed at your table.

# # #

Located just a few blocks away is another Baltimore landmark. The **Old Lexington Market** is the last place most people think about for lunch. But if a little sawdust on the floor and standing at an old wooden bar don't turn you off while really fresh oysters, shrimp and crab turn you on, then try something earthy and original.

Faidley's Raw Bar is tucked in one corner of this large market specializing in everything. Here you can watch your oysters being shucked or select your own crab or jumbo shrimp for a succulent seafood feast. Not only is the price the best in town, but the atmosphere is reeking with nostalgia.

Colorful fruit and vegetable stalls compete for the freshest, cleanest and largest of the popular items while some feature hard to find items such as freshly ground horseradish, coconut and ginger root.

In this day of prepackaged foods it is refreshing to see so many bulk items. Sauerkraut and pickels are weighed by the pound in old galvanized scales. Various types of cottage cheese are sold from large bins at the buttermilk bar.

For a bar in unexpected quarters, visit **Peabody's Book Shop and Beer Stube**. Just Nort of Mt. Vernon Street at 913 N. Charles Street you'll find one of the few (maybe the only) book shop drinking room in the nation. Renowned as the place where H. L. Mencken did much of his writing, this unique bar and upstairs restaurant has been drawing crowds since the 1920's. Tucked in the midst of handsome townhouses, ivy-covered mansions and cathedral spires, this small hole in the wall is an anachronism. I really don't think many go for the worn volumes on the cluttered shelves and heaven knows how Mencken wrote there, it's so dark, but it does have atmosphere and it is fun!

As you leave Peabody's, take a look at the dramatic skyline. Towers, steeples, domes and cupolas interspersed with modern skyscrapers. You'll have to hurry back to discover more inns and eateries of Baltimore.

RICHMOND—A REAL TREASURE TROVE

Richmond is a dynamic city of today, proud of its role in events of yesterday. Its streets are lined with buildings that are monuments to a glorious past. But more exciting to me than the illustrious shrines and famous battle grounds is the current pulse of Richmond. I discovered a fascinating museum, some unique restaurants, a picturesque cottage and a lavish hotel lobby retaining romance of the Deep South—I discovered the red carpets of Richmond.

The Jefferson is the oldest hotel in Virginia and its lobby is majestic. Dominating this turn-of-the-century extravaganza is the dramatic red velvet staircase filmed in the great epic "Gone With The Wind." Lunch on the mezzanine is relaxed and gracious. While you sip a frosted mint julep, marvel at the festooned marble columns, the damask-like walls and elaborately carved ceilings. As you relish country ham and beaten biscuits, revel in the crisp pink linens, sparkling crystal and ornate silver. Inquire about their newly decorated rooms. For a change of pace from modern motels, you might enjoy a night in this renowned hotel of yesteryear.

For another pace-change, visit Sam Millers Exchange Cafe. Once an old grain warehouse, this unique restaurant is a delightful mixture of today and yesterday. Today with its twinkling ticker tape flashing current rates of the New York stock market—yesterday with its old brick walls and pegged pine floors. Today with its mod rock music—yesterday with its church pew benches and cathedral chandeliers. Today with its swift salads, sandwiches and quiche—

yesterday with its massive oak bar and chalkboard menu. Today and yesterday with its copious use of plants and greenery—in the windows, on the walls and even hanging from the high old wooden rafters. It's a fun spot for lunch any day.

You'll find "Poor Richards" equally appealing, especially if you enjoy al fresco dining. An intimate brick patio is a shaded delight in spring and summer. And a heating element in the trees warms the crisp air of autumn days. Old gas lanterns illumine the charming garden at night. Copious drinks are served in pretty crystal, and last but not least, the food is good!

Tucked in the midst of handsome homes, Federal buildings and modern structures, a tiny stone cottage stands out in sharp contrast. The Poe Museum built around 1685, is the oldest house in Richmond. Actually, this miniature facade is one of four buildings opening on to a beautiful walled garden. The entire complex has recently been dedicated as a shrine to one of Richmond's favorite residents, Edgar Allen Poe. Many original manuscripts and various items associated with the famous poet's life are housed here. Of particular interest is a scale model of Richmond as it appeared during Poe's residence in the city.

Highlighting this unusual house is The Raven Room. Black and white ink drawings line blood red walls. A stuffed animal under the portrait of the tragic poet add a poignant note to the stark chamber with its dark wooden floors. The Poe museum on Main Street could easily be overlooked, but is well worth looking for.

Even if you aren't a museum fancier, you will be fascinated with the Virginia Museum of Fine Arts. The entrance is spectacular. A mammoth bronze chandelier hangs above a double, red-carpeted, circular staircase leading to a dramatic hall of tapestries.

The huge edifice is built around two magnificent courts. The Mediterranean Court simulates a Roman atrium with pools, fountains and sculptures.

42

Galleries representing ancient culture surround the court: the Oriental World, Egypt, India and the Classical World (Greece and Rome). Surrounding the Ranaissance Court which resembles an Italian Palace are rooms representing the arts of the modern world. There is even a gallery devoted to the Art Nouvean movement. Strolling through the museum is like visiting a palatial home. Instead of stark halls with art displays, the rooms are tastefully decorated and the paintings on the walls are enhanced by fine furniture and decorative arts representative of the area. Soft background music adds still another pleasurable dimension.

One gallery contains a rare collection of Fabregé jewelry, elaborate Imperial Easter eggs and ornate "objects of fancy." Adjoining each gallery is a tiny orientation theatre where one can press a button and see a color film on the culture and art of the area or period represented.

Meticulous attention to detail throughout the museum particularly impressed me. For instance, the Ancient section is designed to resemble the interior of a pyramid tomb. The Medieval section is built on the lines of a Gothic Cathedral.

In addition to the vast permanent collection and spacious loan gallery, the Virginia Museum offers a full range of cultural activities. There are classes in art, art history and crafts. A library and a 500-seat theatre offer year-round programs of drama, music, dance, cinema and lectures. The Virginia Museum of Fine Arts is in reality a panorama of world art spanning the history of man's creative achievements.

Richmond is a thriving city, nurturing the progress of today while preserving the heritage of the past.

43

MILWAUKEE AND OSHKOSH
—YOU GOTTA BE KIDDING!

I HADN'T PLANNED TO WRITE about Milwaukee and Oshkosh. They were just stops on my way to Wisconsin's Door Peninsula. However, one day and night in each area convinced me these towns are really what "Cozy Getaways" are all about.

Reading facts about Milwaukee evokes a picture of heavy industry and factories 'midst fumes of beer. Actually, this vibrantly progressive city presents a different scene entirely. An impressive skyline against the west shores of Lake Michigan is studded with church spires, domes, cupolas and towers. These notable sanctuaries, along with fascinating architecture and colorful restaurants, reflect the diversified ethnic origins of the city.

I once read that Milwaukee had no deluxe hotels. Frankly, I'd rate the Pfister right with the best. I didn't check out the new round tower, but rooms in the old section are large and gracious. A beautiful view and good combo make an evening on the roof memorable and for French toast, I'd walk that proverbial mile to their Coffee Shop. (Really, it's the best I've ever eaten.)

Art centers, museums, conservatories and parks enhance the cultural significance of Milwaukee. A three and a half mile lakefront residential area is one of the loveliest in the nation.

The Boerner Botanical Gardens in picturesque Whitnall Park are really beautiful. Fourteen miles of nature trails wind through native woodlands. For the golfer there's an 18-hole course. Picnic areas are strategically located amidst

44

rock gardens, pools and fountains. Formal gardens punctuate this floral wonderland with a profusion of seasonal blooms. Roses numbering some 5000 are bordered by colorful annuals and perennials. Regardless of the season, you will enjoy an interlude of relaxation and inspiration in these scenic gardens.

A thoroughly exhilarating horticultural experience awaits your visit to the city's unique conservatory. Three huge glass beehive domes are the setting for fabulous displays of exotic trees, plants and flowers from all over the world. A dramatic 25-foot waterfall highlights the lush tropical house. Growth arrangements from towering 70-foot palms to creeping, verdant ground cover create a true tropical forest. Orchids, hibiscus, water lilies and birds add the finishing touch.

I found the arid house particularly exciting. This dome houses a desert with an amazing array of cacti and succulents, fantastically arranged in a setting of massive man-made rock.

The third dome is the showhouse where seasonal floral exhibits are staged—really sensational productions. This has got to be the best show in town for only thirty-five cents.

A drive through nearby Washington Heights is like driving through several European villages. You see charming homes with turrets and cobblestoned entryways. The influence of Gothic, Teutonic, Norman and Victorian architecture results in an unusual melange of styles.

In a city noted for German restaurants, two are spectacular—Ratzsch's and Maders. It would be hard to say which has more old-world charm and atmosphere. Both serve superb food in a Bavarian style setting amidst fabulous collections of antiques. Both have wine lists so extensive it would take an evening to peruse.

Ratzsch's features a Viennese string ensemble. Maders is located in a small medieval castle and has a fascinating gift shop. You must go to each—but not in the same day. That's just too much of a good thing. And oh, those Germanic calories!

Speaking of calories, across the street from Maders is the colorful Usinger's factory and retail store. Famous for almost a hundred years for quality sausage products, Usinger's retains the charm of a bygone era in its old-world recipes and decorative murals both inside and outside of the picturesque example of 16th century German architecture.

Continuing my journey to the Door Peninsula, I stopped overnight at Oshkosh. Ten feet from its shores is a tiny self-contained island in Lake Winnebago. Pioneer Inn caters to vacationers seeking solitude as well as those looking for action. Yes, it's possible in this small world of luxury and fun to commune with nature or join in swinging festivities. A rustic two-storied structure has spacious rooms, some of which overlook the lake. Those on the Fox River are the most private. Three restaurants and two intimate lounges provide gourmet dining and entertainment year-round.

Activities are determined by the weather. Pick your season, then take your pick. There's a marina for boating, fishing and water skiing. Besides the lake, both heated indoor and outdoor pools lure swimmers. Nearby you'll find tennis, golf, horseback riding, bicycling and seasonal hunting. Snowmobiling, ice-boating, ice-skating, broom hockey, ice-fishing and skiing are offered in the winter.

The Grey Fox, right over the bridge, is a delightful restaurant on the Park Plaza Mall terrace. Its sidewalk cafe with modernistic lamp-posts and large concrete planters of flowers looks out over the Fox River and Marina. You can't imagine the beer and ale list. Beer from Mexico, Finland, Denmark, Austria—you name it, it's there, even one from Japan.

Walter von Gunten lives and does his thing in Oshkosh. "Scherenschnitte" is his specialty. Yes, the spelling is correct and translated it means "scissor cutting." He has revived and updated the ancient art of wielding tiny sharp sewing scissors to create intricate designs. Von Gunten has had many exhibits throughout the States, appeared on TV and been featured in newspapers and magazines. You can visit his studio, by appointment, and view or purchase his unique works.

Dan Dee Vue Farms has turned an old barn into an antique shop. Not far away is the Cabin Candle Shop and in a beautiful English Mansion on Algoma Boulevard surrounded by formal gardens you'll find the Paine Art Center.

Sometimes, cities are not what they seem. If you've always associated Oskhosh with luggage and Milwaukee with beer and baseball, just take a look around. Find those special churches, tranquil parks, enticing restaurants and remarkable architecture. Milwaukee and Oshkosh can be cozy getaways—no kidding.

SANTA FE—WONDROUSLY DIFFERENT

NEW MEXICO'S SCENIC GRANDEUR is startling. Its surviving scene of Indian and Spanish culture is remarkable. Surely no area of North America presents such a strikingly varied panorama. Majestic snow-capped mountains, tiny Indian pueblos and charming adobe architecture of age-old Spanish towns combine to make New Mexico a perfect place to relive yesterday in the splendor of today.

Santa Fe lies in the North Central section of this golden land. Framed by the towering Sangre de Cristo mountains, this fascinating city with its low, thick-walled adobe buildings and narrow, brick-paved streets seems to echo tones of surging serenity. Rosy tan hues of distinctive adobe and wood construction reflect a warmth and individuality innate to this oldest state capital, founded in 1610. Typically old west, Santa Fe is at the same time singularly Spanish with a central Plaza pulsating at the heart of town.

From 1821 until the arrival of the railroad, this picturesque Plaza marked the end of the fabled Santa Fe trail. Today, encircled by art galleries, museums, restaurants and shops, all housed in historic old buildings, it is the focal point for both townspeople and tourists. Under the long, graceful *portales* of the Palace of the Governors, colorfully dressed Indians from surrounding pueblos sell their jewelry and pottery. The Palace is the oldest public building in the United States in continuous use. It seems an appropriate marketplace for these beautiful Indians, who were so proud of their land long before Conquistadores intruded,

48

to display their ancient arts and crafts.

Competing for brilliance with the legendary skies of New Mexico is the turquoise, coral and silver Indian jewelry. Each unique shop has an inexhaustible supply of heshi, squash blossoms and trading beads. Quality is the trademark at Rivera's. Each Rivera piece is individually designed. Pottery, nambé, hand-loomed items and art are also among New Mexico's good buys.

Shady, winding streets and bracingly cool, dry air make walking a pleasant way to savor the delights of Santa Fe. A few blocks from the center of town unpaved roads curve along streams. Bordering cottonwood trees grace streets lined with adobe homes.

Old missions, chapels and churches (including a Romanesque Cathedral) add a spiritual dimension to this ageless city which so reveres tradition. The Mission of San Miguel, the oldest church in America, and the Church of Cristo Rey are outstanding examples of Spanish mission architecture.

St. Francis Cathedral and tiny Loretto Chapel, steeped in curiously intriguing histories, reveal an incongruous architectural profile. The Cathedral was built under the direction of Archbishop John Baptist Lamy, made famous in Willa Cather's book "Death Comes to the Archbishop." The Gothic stone chapel houses the fabled "Miraculous Staircase." When the chapel was completed there was no means of ascending to the choir loft. A mysterious carpenter appeared, constructed a circular staircase built without nails or any visible means of support, then disappeared. Legend persists it was the work of St. Joseph, the carpenter saint.

Along Canyon Road, formerly an old Indian trail, flat-roofed adobe structures with gentle arches and romantic courtyards have been converted into art galleries, studios, shops, boutiques, bistros and restaurants. Here you'll find The Compound, one of my all-time favorites. Unusually decorated in beige and white, this elegant restaurant epitomizes the ultimate in ambience, service and continental cuisine.

The Palace, near Santa Fe Plaza, is another superb restaurant. Its luxurious decor is reminiscent of the Victorian era. An attractive restored Western saloon adjoins. The Bull Ring is a rambling area of bars, patios and dining rooms *on Old Santa Fe Trail*. It offers a classic French menu. If Mexican food is your fancy, try The Paragua located in Española, 15 miles north of Santa Fe—it's great, with loads of atmosphere.

Santa Fe has many accommodations with local color. Some have unique corner fireplaces indigenous to this section. La Posada Inn, Desert Inn, La Fonda, Hilton and Inn Loretto are in the center of town. The new Sheraton nestled high above Santa Fe affords a spectacular view. Several Ranch-Inns a few miles out of town provide an enchanting setting with many forms of recreation. Rancho Encantado and Bishops Lodge are just minutes away in Tesque.

The 65-mile drive North to Taos is dazzling—an illusion of a collage with wind-sculptured rock cliffs, snowy mountain peaks and deep gorges. It's an escape into a timeless land where values and pace are not measured by ordinary standards. People in these remote mountain villages live much as their ancestors did.

At first glance Taos appears to be an overgrown pueblo, but it is actually a rare combination of primitive and sophisticated cultures. Artists and writers have adopted this town as their own. It has retained a completely original Spanish character, hard to find in North America. Art galleries abound. Shops featuring local handicrafts offer diversion for those not devoting every minute to the ski slopes.

The Sagebrush Inn is beautiful. Typifying the mood and style of the area, it commands an unsurpassed view and offers convenience and good food in a gracious setting.

Taos has several small but outstanding restaurants. La Doña Luz, an adobe home built in 1802, is now a charming spot to eat (and drink). Mary and Bob Clark, the owners, take as much pride in their community as in the food and wine they serve in their colorful restaurant. Happy to help with sightseeing and shopping trips, they told us not to miss Taos Indian Pueblo and the village of Chimayo and Trampas.

Three miles North of Taos is one of the most remarkably preserved of New Mexico's 19 Indian pueblos. It retains a fortress-like appearance with impressive five-storied "apartment buildings" made of adobe and mud. Outdoor ovens resembling beehives are still used for baking bread. This makes it all the more surprising to see TV antennas. But to see ancient mixed with modern is not so unique. The Indians live in these pueblos (a Spanish word meaning "community") occupying almost the same lands which the Indians held during the early Spanish occupation.

By returning to Santa Fe on back roads (Routes 3 and 76), we passed through a chain of miniature hamlets terraced into the niches of the mountainside. Chimayo, home of the famed Chimayo blankets, seemed the most unlikely place in the world to find a healing font. But a legend of miraculous cures has turned El Santurario, originally a private chapel, into the Lourdes of New Mexico. Here even skeptics feel a special quiescence pervading the air.

Someone has said this land of enchantment remains America's best-guarded secret. The State motto, "Cresit erundo," (it grows and goes) sums up the climate, the character and the philosophy of Santa Fe.

From ATOP THE 607 FOOT HIGH Space Needle, Seattle looms vast and vibrant. Ships, ferries and sailboats play their roles on the magnificent stage of myriad waterways. Olympic Mountains to the West and mighty snow-peaked Mt. Ranier to the East create a dazzling backdrop.

Legendarily, Seattle like Rome, is built on seven hills. (As you are walking or driving, you'll declare it's closer to 70.) From the Space Needle's slowly revolving restaurant, you can "explore" the city's sights and sidetrips. This is one sightseeing spot where food and beverages live up to the view. Brunch is served from 9am to 3pm daily and fanciful drinks and desserts are featured from 3pm 'til dinner. A compass-like needle on the menu locates the chief points of interest of the city.

The waterfront teems with activity. Sightseeing boats cruise the harbor hourly. Ferries sail to Victoria, Vancouver and the Puget Sound Islands. The city's fishing fleet and dock yards are a-bustle early. Marinas harbor thousands of boats. (You can charter one with or without a crew.) A maze of colorful restaurants and import shops are part of the exciting waterfront scene.

A good approach to the waterfront is via the Pike Place Market where farmers used to sell their fresh produce from wagons. Today, it is a covered marketplace for fresh fruits, vegetables, fresh and salt-water fish, arts, crafts and antiques—a real shopping experience.

The University of Washington on the shores of Lake Washington is situated in one of the largest and most beautiful sections of the city. Its arboretum boasts a four-acre Japanese tea garden. Theaters, shops, museums and ethnic restaurants add an international dimension to this park-like campus.

Pioneer Square is the oldest neighborhood in Seattle. Here the original pioneers drove their first stakes for a lumber town which burned in 1889. With resurging nostalgia, this "skidroad" area is being restored. Two-level arcades with gourmet restaurants and specialty shops amid little parks make this a great walking place. For riders, Seattle offers a unique service—free downtown buses.

On one of the city's highest hills you'll encounter Chinatown—officially designated as the International District. You'll love browsing in its oriental shops, galleries and museums. Have fun choosing from the many excellent Chinese and Japanese restaurants. You can't go wrong with Bush Gardens or The Four Seas.

The World's Fair of 1962 bequeathed to Seattle a home for the performing arts—an arena, playhous and opera house. Among the fascinating facilities in this large complex are an International Bazaar, an art museum pavillion, a craft center, a stadium and the Drydock Restaurant. In less than two minutes the Monorail whisks you between the Center and downtown.

The Olympic Hotel remains regally elegant, yet with an upbeat mood. It's unfortunate that tall buildings have obstructed its once superb view of the harbor. For a room with a view, you'll love Edgewater Inn. It extends out over the water. You can literally catch a fish out of your window and have the chef cook your catch for dinner.

If you are interested in fresh salmon barbequed Indian style over alderwood, don't bypass Ivar's Salmon House on the North Shore of Lake Union. You'll delight in the Indian motif as well as the uniquely flavored salmon.

Sensational sidetrips from Seattle are numerous and varied. Snoqualmie Falls Lodge is about 30 miles North. Perched atop a waterfalls higher than Niagara, this popular inn has been serving "farm breakfasts" and "country dinners" since 1916.

Soaring to 14,412 feet, Mt. Ranier is the reigning queen over Seattle's southern horizon. Glistening white in the sun's rays, shading to mauve as it is enveloped by twilight, Mt. Ranier is a constant magnet to everyone within its visual orbit. A three-hour drive from Seattle takes you to Mt. Ranier National Park. Towering snow-capped peaks are reflected in shimmering lakes. Trails weave through meadows lush with alpine flowers, rugged with dense timber and fresh with waterfalls and glacial streams.

West of Seattle, across Puget Sound, lies the unspoiled wilderness of the Olympic Peninsula, a utopia for hikers and skiers. Rain forests contrast sharply with distant icy glaciers. Lakes and streams provide great fishing. There are a few hotels, cabins and campsites in the picturesque coastal towns. For rest and relaxation, you can't beat the natural mineral waters at Sol Duc Hot Springs.

To really get away from it all, go to Neah Bay. Your excursion to the outermost point of the State of Washington includes a ferry ride and miles of spectacular scenery. Wildlife in dense woodlands, an abandoned Indian village, a fishing fleet, and carved totem poles are among the fascinating attractions in this remote wonderland. Salmon fishing is great in the countless streams. So are shells and driftwood along sandy beaches.

Hundreds of wooded, mountainous isles in the seas between the Cascades and Olympic Mountain make up the San Juan Islands. Discovered in the late 1700's, this lovely island archipelago remains virtually unspoiled. From Whidbey, the largest island, to tiny, lofty spired humps, each island exudes its own unique charm. Some have gently sloping beaches, others have fjords that rival those of Norway. The larger ones contain inns, small resorts and housekeeping cabins. Make the circuit on the mail boat MV Bristol and discover your own favorite getaway. For peace and seclusion it can't be beat.

Mountains, an ocean shore, lakes, streams, rivers, wildlife, forests of giant trees, boats, ferries, islands and parks—these scenic wonders sum up Seattle's sights and sidetrips.

Islands
to Escape From it All

THE MOMENT YOU STEP ON THE SOIL of St. Croix and take a deep breath of the incredibly clear air, you sense a feeling of physical well-being and serenity. A unique stone sugar mill or an occasional old windmill remind you that St. Croix' history is steeped in diversity. Varied architecture recalls the Danish, French, Dutch and Spanish influences that have molded the personality of this colorful sun-bathed island.

Largest of the U.S. Virgin Islands, St. Croix maintains an easy, relaxed pace while offering varied activities and entertainment appealing to all tastes. Bordering a crystal clear, coral-reefed harbor, Christiansted, the island's capital, epitomizes tropical graciousness. Brilliant bougainvillea and hibiscus embroider beautifully preserved 18th century buildings. Tracery of wrought iron gates frame glimpses of romantic courtyards. Covered sidewalks, colonnades with charming shops and outdoor cafes invite leisurely strolling and shopping.

Merchandise and prices in all the shops are attractive. I found the sales personnel in The Continental on King St. so accommodating that I bought my entire $200 duty free quota right there. The inventory of Lladro and Lalique is unsurpassed. Royal Worcester egg coddlers and maxims make excellent gifts for any occasion. You will also find jewelry, French perfume and men and women's fashions.

The Sun and Moon's advertisements advise you to "travel light ahd heavy up" at their shop in the Pan Am Pavillion. A wide choice of round-the-clock fashions makes it possible to do just that. The boutiques at The Buccaneer and Beach Hotels feature an outstanding selection of bathing suits and long dresses. These two hotels share the same hairdresser. For some intriguing stories about the island and its interesting people while being stylishly coiffed, be sure to ask for Marjorie Rommel, the manager. For a variety of authentic Crucian arts and crafts made on the island with native materials, stop at one of the craft centers on Church Street.

Good restaurants are almost as plentiful as exciting duty-free shopping in Christiansted. The Comanche Terrace overlooking the yacht-filled harbor is a favorite of the locals as well as visitors. Guthrie's in the Holger Danski Hotel has a view and an unusual menu of hamburgers from around the world. Try one with mozzarella cheese and Italian sauce on Italian bread—yummy! A strolling guitarist adds romance to candlelight dining in a delightful patio at La Chitarra behind Jelthrup's Book Shop on King Cross Street. The Steak House at the top of St. Croix-by-the-Sea affords a spectacular view of St. Croix' shoreline and Sunday brunch at Canebay Plantation on the North Shore is really special.

Many excellent hotels are located throughout the island. For something new under the sun, take a look at The Jockey Club on the Cay. This tiny island, just a two-minute boat ride from Christiansted's wharf, is a beautiful resort world all to itself. View the bustling town from your private beach or balcony.

Smaller and quieter, Frederiksted stretches along the waterfront at the western end of the island. Wide, tree-shaded streets are lined with Victorian gingerbread built on top of old Danish buildings. Fort Frederik, built in 1760, is being restored as an historical site and museum.

The drive along Mahogany Road is lushly tropical—a mini rain forest of mahogany and mango trees, palms, papayas, ferns and hanging lianas. On this scenic road you will see a small sign—"Life & Environmental Arts Project." Here, on a mountainside, is an unusual enterprise headed up by a most unique individual. You must stop, meet Fletcher Pence and see first-hand his masterpieces. They are truly poetry in wood. Without the benefit of polished and carpeted display rooms you will see in the raw the artistry of mahogany and thibet (the native hardwoods) in virtually every form—from tables of all types and sizes to candleholders and cutting boards. Most of it will be in process as you watch native and stateside apprentices learning the art as Mr. Pence attempts to promote the local economy by passing down his skills. I guarantee you will not find two identical pieces since Fletcher's philosophy is that the wood dictates the shape and form. And don't forget, no export duty is charged on Virgin Island made goods, so whatever you buy here is duty free.

Between Frederiksted and Christiansted are many old plantations, churches and sights worth seeing. Whim Greathouse is a real showplace. A museum of a house typifying the grand style of sugar planters in the 1700's at the peak of St. Croix' prosperity. Recently rebuilt, the sails of its great windmill turn in the tradewinds to operate the sugar grinding machinery. Geared to today's tempo, the Island Center is a miniature cultural center where you can enjoy music, theatre and art in various forms.

Buck Island, with its glorious border of white sandy beach, is a highlight not to be missed. Three miles northeast of Christiansted, Buck Island, a national park, is accessible only by boat. Even non-swimmers can enjoy the fabulous spectacle of corals, fishes, sponges and myriad species of undersea life which make this one of the world's outstanding snorkeling spots. Whatever else you do, pack a picnic and sail the tradewinds to beautiful Buck Island.

The miracle of St. Croix is more than its story-book villages with quaint shops and restaurants; more than its luxury hotels and bargain buys; more than its beautiful hills and valleys studded with jewel-like homes overlooking white beaches and dazzling blue water with multi-colored coral relief. The miracle is an intangible reality—an up-to-date ... but let me tell you in the words of my friend, Deana Smith, who has experienced the miracle! Here is her story!

"We fell in love with St. Croix years ago as the ideal spot for a vacation in the sun (temperature year-round reaches a high of 86-88° and a low of 65°, with no rainy season). But it was only in November of 1972, when I fled to St. Croix after a year of excruciating pain, surgery and long sojourns in hospital, that I began to realize the unique abilities of the climate to work miracles. I became fascinated with the subject and research verified that many people had enjoyed the same, almost instantaneous relief from pain and a resurgence of the joy of living. My neurosurgeon has verified that the steady barometric pressure in St. Croix (it never varies more than one-tenth of one percent) is responsible for the "miracle." It doesn't effect a permanent cure, but a month to six weeks there enables me to function normally at home for about three months, whereas in the past I had been incapacitated 50 to 75 percent of the time.

"I became so excited about my discovery that I interviewed numerous people who found relief in St. Croix from crippling arthritis, rheumatism, other joint and back problems, heart problems, migraine headaches, even post-nasal drip! Following are some of the more exciting and dramatic cures I unearthed.

"One woman who had suffered from arthritis for years bought a home in St. Croix and recovered so completely that she decided to travel around the world and find other places where she could enjoy the same benefits. Six years later after trying every type of climate and location, she was settled permanently in St. Croix and says she will never leave again.

"Another couple visited friends in St. Croix for Christmas three years ago. The wife, in misery with arthritis, declared after a week that she would never leave and she is now a happy native.

61

"A friend who had suffered back pain most of his adult life tried many locations. Sixteen years ago he moved to St. Croix, started his own accounting firm, and has led a useful and productive life every since.

"I interviewed an artist who has become famous for his beautiful back painting on glass and learned that he moved to St. Croix when his hands became so crippled from arthritis that he could neither paint nor continue his original work as an architect. Eventually I realized why so many artists live in St. Croix—they are able to continue painting.

"One young girl told me she had been desperately ill with asthma when her parents persuaded her to try St. Croix. She is now holding a responsible position with one of the largest condominium developments on the island.

"Then there is the gentleman who arrived in a wheelchair, emaciated and racked with the pain of rheumatism. The wheelchair has long since disappeared and he has returned to his normal weight and everyone swears he looks at least thirty years younger.

"One heart specialist has become so sold on the therapeutic values of the St. Croix climate that he orders many of his patients to recuperate there.

"But to me the most dramatic miracle of St. Croix is mine. That is the "proof of the pudding." After 12 years of traction, operations, physical therapy and an operation to remove a disintegrated disc which damaged the nerve so badly that I had a dropped foot, I went to St. Croix. Thirty pounds overweight from edema produced by massive doses of cortisone, I didn't care whether I lived or died. Ten days later I was going to parties, shopping and beginning to enjoy life again. The edema flowed out of me as if a balloon had been pricked. Since then, it's been UP all the way. I swim, sail, dance and enjoy life to the hilt. I'm convinced that I'll live to a ripe old—active—age, enjoying the endless facets of St. Croix life, traveling to far places and knowing that I can always return to the Miracle of St. Croix."

That is Deana's wonderful story, but not necessarily the end. She and I had lunch the other day at The Comanche. Deana has just about convinced me to buy one of the attractive villas at The Reef on Teague Bay. You can't find a more desirable place to live or visit in St. Croix. A self-contained resort complex on a hillside, The Reef boasts a private white sand beach, a golf course, swimming pool, sauna, tennis courts, boating and fishing. If you get there, give Deana a call—maybe she will convince *you* to share in the Miracle of St. Croix.

HIGH ATOP MAJESTIC CLIFFS a dramatic lighthouse beckons you to an island of unspoiled, uncluttered and untouristed natural wilderness. Daily tempo on Grand Manan in New Brunswick, Canada, is so leisurely, that if you miss the Sunday morning (7:30 am) ferry to the mainland, you remain on the island 'til Monday. But that's not a bad idea anyway. Sunday on Grand Manan is just about as relaxed and far away from it all as you can get. Life continues pretty much the same here as it has for the last fifty years or more.

To reach Grand Manan, take the auto ferry from Black's Harbour on Route 1 in Southeast New Brunswick. It takes one hour and 45 minutes to cross Fundy Bay. Although there are no towns, no organized activities, very few places to stay and practically no shops or restaurants, you will find plenty to do; that is, if you enjoy a vacationer's vacation—doing nothing.

The scenery on Grand Manan is striking. The air is clean and crisp. Green waters of Fundy Bay break gently on sandy beaches along the Eastern shores, while surf on the Western coast pounds onto craggy, steep bluffs. Paved roads wind around storm-sculptured rock formations, through groves of spruce and pine trees, and along picturesque coves and harbors. Thousands of sea birds, lobster pots and herring weirs accentuate the panoramic seascapes. Boats converge around fish-stands built on high stilts. Very few places in the world experience such a range of tides—up to 40 feet. During low tide, you can literally walk on the floor of the ocean. "The Thoroughfare" leads to Ross Island, site of

Grand Manan's first settlement in 1784.

Fishing settlements dot the peaceful shores. Ever since the days following the Revolution when fleeing Loyalists settled Grand Manan, Scotch and English descendants have sought their livelihood from the abundant sea. Herring is the big catch.

A rich, tangy aroma permeates the air around Seal Cove where weather-beaten herring houses are veiled in hickory smoke. The silvery, slim herrings can be seen through slits in the walls and sea gulls love to perch on the rooftops.

Would you believe that in the herring capital of the world, I couldn't find a single smoked herring. I also struck out on lobster. There is a massive lobster pound, but from July to November it's empty! Some lobsters have been frozen for use in soups and chowders, but even those are scarce by mid-September. What I missed in lobster I made up for with home-baked rolls and pie. Most of the inns and cabins are family owned and operated. The Grand Manan islanders love to cook and take pride in their meals. Food is good and prices are reasonable.

They eat early on Grand Manan—6:00 pm period. No cocktail lounges or bars. One liquor store. One or two carryout spots. Evening entertainment includes watching a beautiful sunset and exchanging travel experiences with other guests in front of a cherry fire in the fall or on a shaded verandah in the summer. "Oh, it's the courage and friendliness of the islanders that lures us back each year," a passenger on the ferry confided to me. "This is our fifth trip. Nowhere have we found more tranquility and hospitality." I tend to agree.

Although the island is small (16 miles long and 6 wide), distances are important. If you really need to make the 7:30 am ferry, it behooves you to put your car in line around 5:00 pm the evening before. This means you have to walk back to your lodgings, then retrace your steps early the next morning. The Marathon Hotel is just a few yards from the dock. Shore Crest Lodge is nearby and Surfside is .7 of a mile. To stay farther out, you must know someone with a car, (to taxi you to and from yours) or keep your schedule flexible.

The best looking place on the island with an unsurpassed view is Ocean View Lodge. Nurses at the front desk smilingly told me this was a nursing home and suggested several places for me to try. At Whale Cove, a few quaint, gray cottages were covered with scarlet vines. Willa Cather was inspired in this secluded spot to write several of her books.

The Marathon Hotel, built by a retired sea captain, is a delightful old white clapboard Inn. Its rooms are spotlessly spic and span. I opted for one with a view instead of a private shower. Quite frankly, sharing a bathroom isn't my idea of "atmosphere" so the next day I made a shift. Rooms at Surfside are small, but have a private bath, TV and are right on the edge of the water.

With no demands on your time, you can enjoy miles of scenic hiking and biking trails on Grand Manan. You can explore caves or climb out on promontories of rugged land with sheer drops to the Atlantic. Church spires, fishing villages, lighthouses and wind-sculptured rocks resembling cathedrals, castles and figments of an active imagination keep cameras clicking. The Anchorage is a mecca for bird watchers—a sanctuary for more than 250 varieties of birds. Most of these are preserved at the Grand Manan Museum.

Charter boats are available for deep sea fishing and excursions. The island lakes are stocked with bass and trout. On all day boat trips around the island a special lunch of hot chowder is included. To view Grand Manan from the sea and to leisurely savor its old world tempo is to capture a bit of serenity—a memorable experience.

Villages with a Tang of Salt in the Air

IV

FISHING VILLAGES ARE FASCINATING; none more so than in the captivating area of Cape Ann. Situated 50 miles north of Boston, Cape Ann is a rock-lined coast of natural beauty, studded with sandy beaches and linked with a chain of picturesque towns.

Rockport and Gloucester, almost overlapping at the tip of the Cape, snuggle close to their sparkling harbors. Fishing still flourishes in these historic seaports, but artists and writers now outnumber the colorful old fishermen.

Lighthouses, lobster shacks, old schooners and a multiformity of architecture compete for the artist's palette. Fresh native fish, clams, scallops and lobsters galore pamper gourmet's palate. Quaint shops, antiques, art galleries and historic buildings lure the sight-seers. Bird sanctuaries, gardens and massive rock formations appeal to nature lovers. Sailing, skiing, fishing and swimming are for sports enthusiasts. Here is a total getaway—something for everyone.

Rockport is a perfect base from which to explore this unique region. Delightful inns, guest homes and motels abound: some are tucked in tiny coves, some face the broad blue sea and others are perched high atop moss-covered boulders.

Captain's Bounty Motor Inn is ideally located on the beach. It is within walking distance of specialty shops and galleries. Across the street is the Peg Leg Restaurant, a great place for breakfast. (Be sure to try their country sausage and fresh blueberry muffins.) All rooms have balconies with a spectacular view and a few are complete with a stove and big cooking pots! This is worth the small additional charge if you like to boil your own freshly caught lobster (undoubtedly the least expensive way to enjoy this succulent treat).

Sidewalk shops decorate the narrow streets of pictorial Bearskin Neck. They offer the diverse assortment of souvenirs and gifts that everyone looks for when away from home. Don't miss "Serendipity," which features very handsome copper waterfalls and unusual pieces of metal sculpture. The top floor of many of these tiny shops are for rent.

Walking is the best way to enjoy Rockport. Adding color and fun to the scene are harbor boat tours and the leisurely pace of a four-passenger surrey with a fringe on top. Oleana by the Sea and Old Farm Inn are among the many restaurants serving good food. If you enjoy a drink before dinner, remember to take your own. (This applies only to Rockport.)

Scenic Routes 127 and 128 weave north through the quiet, gracious towns of Essex and Ipswich and south through Gloucester, Magnolia and Manchester. Lofty trees shade streets lined with traditional New England clapboard houses. Their diversified colors range from white to charcoal. Trim varies from muted tones of blue to shades of shocking pink.

Outcroppings of native rock have been converted into lovely terraces and rock gardens. Flowers bloom in profusion and in late May the whole area is ablaze with lilacs. Everywhere you look there are lilacs—lavender, white, pink and deep purple.

Founded in 1633, nearby Ipswich was named after old Ipswich, England. Its ancient Green abounds in history and many outstanding examples of 17th century architecture have been restored by an active historical society. Native clams share in Ipswich's claim to fame. You might try some at Ship Ahoy and Dexter's Hearthside Inn.

For souvenirs and fine furniture indigenous to the area, stop at The Laughing Lion woodworking mill at the junction of Routes IA and 133, which reproduces early American pine pieces dating from the early 1800's.

Traveling south, alternate Route 127 follows the sea into Gloucester. Although small, Gloucester is a city of many facets. For many the focal point is the main waterfront. This is Harbor Cove, America's oldest and most historic fishing port. The courage of the Gloucester mariner is a proud page of American history. It is present there today. You can still watch one of the world's great fishing fleets which provides millions of tons of fish for national consumption.

Two of the town's most popular restaurants are located on the waterfront: Gloucester House (terrific mussels) and Captains Courageous. My favorite is a few blocks away—"The Tavern," an all glass dining room overlooking the sea. Equally as alluring in a snow storm as on a sunny day, the Tavern serves lunch all afternoon. You just can't find better baked lobster—it's even stuffed with lobster. And their version of a frosty beer comes in a frost-rimmed mug with a handle so cold you can hardly hang on to it.

East Gloucester, jutting into the harbor, is a mecca for artists and writers. Their thriving art colony is one of the earliest established on the east coast. Galleries, studios, shops and restaurants line the picturesque streets of Rocky Neck. Several modern motels take advantage of the magnificent seascape which includes fishing vessels, light houses and surf.

Dominating the "up in town" skyline are twin blue cupolas atop the Church of Our Lady of Good Voyage. They house the first modern carillon in America. The white stucco Moorish-type church is an appropriate shrine to fishermen. A carved fruitwood stature of Our Lady cradling a Gloucester schooner and ship models above the Stations of the Cross serve as reminders that God protects those in peril of the sea.

70

Old stone walls border the rocky shoreline from Gloucester to Magnolia and Manchester. An aura of understated elegance permeates these charming towns. Sprawling verandahs on palatial homes are laced with wisteria and hanging baskets. Beautifully manicured lawns sweep down to the sea.

A medieval castle looms on the horizon. Filled with art and lavish furnishings from nearly every century, flamboyant Hammond Castle is authentic to its last brick brought from Europe. Housing a 10,000 pipe organ, a Roman bath, tropical pool with artificial rain and secret passages, this colossal, fortress-like structure serves as a museum. Tours and organ concerts in its great cathedral hall offer a cultural dimension to the maritime life of this rugged peninsula. Whatever your lifestyle or whichever season, you can't fail to find Cape Ann completely captivating.

NOT A WORD MORE NEED BE WRITTEN extolling the glories of Williamsburg. With the influx of ten million Bicentennial visitors, however, a timely word may be in order about a few nearby places where fun and history merge. They are close enough to stay while exploring early America's historical panorama, yet inviting enough to constitute a total getaway. Norfolk, Newport News and Hampton, just a half hour's drive from Williamsburg, comprise a maritime peninsula of sea, air and space attractions.

An abundance of quality accommodations exist throughout the area. Strawberry Banks, a modern motel with a spectacular view, is ideally located at the approach to Hampton Roads Bridge Tunnel. I counted 23 ships from my window overlooking the Hampton Harbor. After all, the largest naval installation in the world is just around the bend.

The Norfolk Naval Base and Air Station is home port for 118 ships of the Atlantic and Mediterranean Fleet and 32 aircraft squadrons. On a 45-minute narrated bus tour around the base you can see giant aircraft carriers, nuclear submarines, destroyers and supersonic aircraft. Ships and submarines are open to the public on weekends.

Norfolk has some interesting tours, by land as well as by sea. From Scope, the exciting modernistic cultural convention center, you can take a walking tour which includes several of the city's chief points of interest:

St. Paul's Church is the only structure in Norfolk to survive the British bombardment on the eve of the Revolution. A cannon-ball remains embedded in the south wall. The graves of four centuries are shaded by huge oaks and magnolias.

General Douglas MacArthur's burial site is Norfolk's former courthouse. Nine galleries contain exhibits and memorabilia of MacArthur's remarkable career. Walter Cronkite narrates a film on the great General's life.

Walter P. Chrysler gave his world-famous art collection to Norfolk. The Chrysler Museum contains a fabulous collection of cut glass in addition to treasures from the earliest periods of art history to the present.

A drive-it-yourself tour takes you out to Gardens-by-the-Sea. Started in 1936 as a WPA project, Norfolk's Botanical Gardens have grown into 175 gorgeous acres of gardens within a garden. Lakes, ponds, gazebos, windmills, an orchid house and a bird sanctuary enrich the handsomely landscaped arboretum.

A trackless train that runs along 17 miles of pathways and canopied boats that sail along quiet canals are pleasant ways to enjoy the Japanese gardens, the Colonial gardens, a sunken garden, and the fragrance, rose and perennial gardens. Spring's 200,000 blooming azaleas are a colorful living tribute to NATO. Originating in 1954, Norfolk's annual International Azalea Festival salutes the North Atlantic Treaty Organization countries. A tree from each of these countries is planted on the Hill of Nations, where a dramatic observation tower provides a panoramic view of the gardens.

Drive by the Adam Thoroughgood House. Thoroughgood, who is credited with naming Norfolk, came to Virginia as an indentured servant and gained prosperity as a tobacco planter. His house, built in the late 1600's, is one of America's oldest existing brick homes.

The Heritage Foundation Museum, located on the grounds of a grand riverside estate, is decorated with Oriental and Medieval art from many countries and periods. The beautiful park surrounding the mansion is open to the public.

For a hearty and delicious meal one should visit Lockhart's. Located on a busy thoroughfare (8440 Tidewater Drive), Johnny Lockhart's is a restaurant "for those who prefer to cherish life rather than rush thru it." It offers a Siesta menu from noon until midnight. Their *midde'* flaming hot pots are terrific. Try one—oyster, clams, shrimp, scallops, bouillabaise, pot-au-feu or gumbo—you'll like it.

For a gourmet experience in Hampton, I recommend Hispañola. This exceptional seafood restaurant on the waterfront in Old Hampton is built to resemble quaint buildings along an 18th century English waterfront with the Brig "Hispañola" moored in a slip between the shops. Nautical art and artifacts decorate the attractive restaurant and are featured in the adjoining gift shop. A Quarter-Deck Lounge completes the waterfront complex.

Hampton spans the centuries. It is the oldest continuous English-speaking settlement in America. Here also our astronauts learned to walk on the moon. Langley Research Center is part of the National Aeronautic and Space Administration. You can ride on a double-decker English bus through Langley Air Force Base past spheres and wind tunnels where astronauts practices lunar liftoffs. A moon rock, a spacesuit worn by Alan Shepard and the Apollo 12 spacecraft are on exhibit at the Visitor's Center. Here, too, you can see a film showing Hampton's other attractions.

For sports, shows and happenings, the Hampton Coliseum looms dramatically on the horizon. St. John's Church, founded in 1610, is the oldest Anglican parish in America. Its communion silver, made in London in 1618, is considered the most precious relic of the Anglican Church in America. One of the beautiful stained glass windows depicts the baptism of Pocahontas.

Fort Monroe in Hampton is the only fort surrounded by a moat in

America. Lincoln plotted a military campaign here, Lee served here and Confederate President Jefferson Davis was imprisoned here. From the Fort's ramparts you can watch ships navigate the Hampton waters. You can even cruise aboard the Kicotan Clipper to the Norfolk Naval Station and to the Newport News Shipbuilding and Drydock. This is the world's largest shipyard. It has built greats such as the passenger liner United States and the first nuclear powered aircraft carrier, The Enterprise.

Newport News is also home of one of the world's foremost collections of marine artifacts. The Mariners Museum contains an extraordinary collection of ship figureheads and miniature vessels.

A war memorial museum houses a unique assemblage of memorabilia representing every conflict in our country's history from pre-Revolutionary times to Viet Nam. Victory Arch stands in stone as a continuing memorial to all men and women of the Armed Forces.

Close to Williamsburg in distance and heritage, Virginia's Maritime Peninsula brims with man's efforts to explore the deep and subdue the planets while preserving an illustrious past.

 HE FASCINATION OF WINTER ON THE waterfront need not be the exclusive province of artists and writers who have long appreciated quiet, abandoned beaches. It is for anyone who adores surf, sand, and crisp clear air without teeming crowds and neon lights.

The Eastern shores of North Carolina, known as the Outer Banks, are ideal for a winter safari. From the landing of Sir Walter Raleigh's first colony in 1585 to the Wright Brothers short first flight in 1903, this coastal region is steeped in history.

Extending from Kitty Hawk to Cape Fear, the Outer Banks are a maze of scenic inlets, islets, bridges, beaches, dunes, lighthouses and fishing villages. Time, tides and storms have sculptured this narrow 120-mile long strip of sand. The Labrador current meets the Gulf Stream along the Outer Banks, making this one of the few places in the world where you can find both cold-water Maine-type lobster and warm-water langostino. Reason enough to journey in this direction.

Nags Head, located midway in the stretch of barrier islands, is a perfect spot to make your headquarters. From here you can take short excursions or simply revel in peaceful quiescence. Winter weather varies. Some days are warm with a calm sea and blue skies; others are windy and cold with an angry sea and stormy skies. The littoral sands are always a treasureland for shell collectors and driftwood fanciers.

A few motels are open year round. But for the ultimate in privacy and luxury you can't beat "Nags Head Sails," a new ocean-front condominium. Ask any of the rental agencies in town about these tastefully decorated apartments. Some accommodate as many as eight people. Large balconies overlook vast uncluttered beachland.

From these balcony vantage points it is fun to watch hearty, young surfers push their surfboards into the frigid water and glide in on the long Atlantic waves. Sea gulls swoosh by at eye-level. Frequently you will see the impressive spectacle of hundreds of dolphins splashing South.

Seafare is the place to eat. Their she-crab soup is super! And the Galleon Esplanade is the place to shop. From a victorian pawnshop to a continental delicatessen, you'll be delighted with this attractive mini-mall. The Island Gallery and Christmas Shop is as intriguing a shopping complex as you'll find anywhere. Twenty-eight rooms in four connected buildings are filled with glittering trees and decorations and dazzling paintings, sculptures and crafts. (Sorry, but it closes Christmas Eve until March.)

Seaside Gallery has a collection of unusual tables made of driftwood and glass. If you feel inspired to make your own you will find all sorts of exciting driftwood at the Shipwreck. To end your day on a note of conviviality drive to The Ranch at Mile Post 7. That's where the action is throughout the year with music and dancing nightly.

Cape Hatteras is 60 miles south of Nags Head. It is hard to believe that this expansive, unspoiled National Seashore is referred to as "The Graveyard of the North Atlantic." But even the tallest lighthouse on American shores didn't prevent more than 500 ships from floundering and going down off its shoals. Many of the old wrecks can be seen from the shore. Others have been beached and can be explored.

Fishermen found Hatteras long before there were roads. Fishing here knows no season. Some of the finest fishing to be found in the world is in these waters. Offshore, inshore, trolling or bottom fishing in salt or fresh water—it's all here. I especially love to watch the fishermen (and women) casting into the crashing surf. One man told us he caught 150 flounder in just a few hours. Charter boats are available for deep sea fishing. Some of the captains descend from families that have been fishing these waters for over 200 years.

If you don't care to catch and cook your own, you must sample some freshly caught rock or blue fish at one of the small seafood restaurants. Fishermen seem to like the food at "Capt. Peels." Also, be sure to visit the combination tackle and gift shop run by Capt. Peels. If hand-carved gulls and geese strike your fancy, follow the signs to "Carved Birds."

A two-hour ferry ride out of Hatteras lands you at a remote, quaint island. Ocracoke reeks with romantic folklore. Wild ponies roam this tiny island where the oldest lighthouse on the Atlantic Coast is still in service. Blackbeard and his pirates are rumored to have buried some treasure here, so don't be surprised if some of your fellow passengers are carrying shovels. You'd do well to carry along some bread crumbs because the hungry sea gulls who follow the ferry expect a handout.

In addition to sea and shore birds, the Outer Banks abound in winter-resident waterfowl, particularly snow geese, Canadian geese, ducks and whistling swans. Bird watchers will be thrilled with the 6700 acres preserved as a National Wildlife Refuge. Hundreds of species of birds stop here for feeding on their annual migration.

Nature lovers will be equally elated with an everchanging landscape—the dramatic contrast of sparse sea oats and beach grass growing on one side of the road, lush forest on the other side. Pines, beech, holly, gum and dogwood grow in profusion with Spanish moss weeping from some of the wind-stunted trees.

Honoring the birth of aviation, a 60-foot monument is built on the mountainous dune from which Wilbur and Orville Wright piloted their machine. Nearby, a museum houses a reproduction of their plane; the original is on display at the Smithsonian in Washington, D.C.

On North Carolina's Outer Banks, there is enough beauty, fun and educational adventure for your whole family to thoroughly enjoy the winter beach.

CAPE MAY–A COUNTRY TOWN BY THE SEA

CAPE MAY EXUDES A SINGULAR quality. You feel it whether you approach by ferry from Lewes, Delaware, or driving down the Jersey coast through a chain of attractive resort towns. Located on the southernmost point of New Jersey at the confluence of the Delaware Bay and the Atlantic Ocean, Cape May is America's oldest seaside resort. Provincial charm, lacking in other beach towns, characterize this country town by the sea.

Elegant Victorian homes are set back on tree-shaded streets. Engaging architectural styles run rampant—Gothic, Greek revival, Queen Anne, Italiante, Mansard and eclectic. These "gingerbread castles" are regarded of such historical significance that the entire city was placed on the National Register of Historic Places in 1970.

In 1620 (the same year the Mayflower landed at Plymouth) Dutch Captain Cornelius Jacobsen May described the area he gave his name to as "charming climate and fruitful land." Cape May began as a whaling village and grew into a popular "watering place." Reached by stagecoach, steamboat and steam grains, it boasted some of the largest hotels in America. After the great fire of 1878 destroyed everything within 30 acres, Cape May was rebuilt.

You can enjoy walking, biking and carriage tours through this unique National Landmark. The Cape May County Art League sponsors an annual Old House Tour. At this time and also during Victorian Weekend some of the romantic houses of the past and little country churches open their doors to visitors. I fell in love with St. Peters by the Sea. This quaint little blue and white frame church was built in Philadelphia for the 1876 Centennial Exposition. In 1869 it was moved to Cape May Point where it rests in the shadows of Old Point Lighthouse.

The original lighthouse was built in 1744 and at low tide it is possible to see its ruins. The present structure built in 1859, is 165 feet tall. Beaches within its confines are primitive, with high dunes and scrub growth. A nature trail, a bird sanctuary, circular guard towers from World War I and a half-sunken concrete ship from World War II add to the interest of the Point. So does looking for diamonds. Cape May diamonds are semi-precious stones of pure quartz (in shades of amber, pink, blue, green and black) which have been smoothed by the sand and sea.

In the center of Cape May several streets have been converted into a plaza with sidewalk cafes, flowers and an old-fashioned bandstand. Yes, they really stage concerts here, too. A mile and a half promenade along the ocean front is a picturesque setting not only for ocean watching and walking, but for art shows. Held in July, the Promenade Art Show attracts hundreds of fine artists from all over the country.

Totally lacking the honky-tonk trappings of many ocean resorts, Cape May teems with activities and attractions. Modernized Victorian hotels and old guest houses out of the past offer a diversion from the usual motel. As for restaurants, you'll find them on rooftops, waterfronts, and even on porches.

A calm surf, clean white sand and excellent lifeguards have earned Cape May its reputation as one of the finest and safest bathing beaches in the world. Equally spectacular is the fishing. From winter's flounder and cod to summer's bass and blues, you'll find them biting. Commercial skippers seem to have an inside line as to where the big babies swim, so if big game is your idea of fishing, you may want to charter for a day or two.

A landlubber myself, I settled for Axelsson Johnson's Seafood Market. Minus the side effects of seasickness yet absorbing the nautical atmosphere of a real working-fishing dock, this market is engrossing. You can watch fishermen bring in and clean their catch. The selection in October was tremendous and never have I seen such large lobsters. I had to buy a pot big enough to hold them, but with such a delicacy going for $2.75 a pound, it was worth it. In fact, it's worth finding a room with a kitchen just so you can cook your own. Or if you prefer, you can have a picnic and cook it on the beach.

Another interesting fish market is Fisherman's Wharf. Located on picturesque Cape May Harbor, Fisherman's Wharf is good for a whole day's visit. The Lobster House restaurant affords a great view of the harbor and the sharp smell of the sea permeates the premises. Docked alongside the seafood restaurant is the Schooner Americana, a unique floating cocktail lounge. Drinks are served below deck as well as topside. You are called on an intercom when your table is ready. If you had rather shop than drink (or maybe both), The Rigging Loft is crammed with clever gift items. Of course, it's also a treat just to watch the fishing fleet dock and unload a cargo of fresh fish.

Oh, you'll find plenty to do besides sunbathe and swim. Biking is big in Cape May. If you don't carry your wheels with you, there are many for rent. For a change of pace, you might like to go horseback riding. Hidden Valley Ranch is a complete riding academy. MAC (Mid-Atlantic Center for the Arts) schedules a well-rounded program of arts and crafts—even Yoga.

Neighboring towns provide delightful sidetrips. Stone Harbor is my favorite. In Fact, it is so close, I make it headquarters. Undoubtedly the neatest and cleanest beach town I've ever seen, Stone Harber has a few excellent motels and restaurants. Crabbing is particularly good in Stone Harbor. So are bird watching and Italian bread. A large variety of cottages are available monthly or by the season. Some include a boat and private dock. Balconies on the Harbor Towers overlook a nice lagoon. Suites include a living room, two bedrooms and a kitchen (perfect for the lobster cook-in). Further up Route 9, the Tuckahoe Inn is a beautiful place to drive for lunch.

All of Cap May County is vacationland. Prowl its back roads, visit its historic sites, watch an exciting sunset or sunrise, roam around the marinas or walk along miles of beaches. You are bound to sense a very special flavor about Cape May—a country town by the sea.

NEW BRUNSWICK

RAIN LASHING INTO A TURBULENT SEA. Skies brooding. Stores and restaurants on dark, slippery streets closed, battened down for a storm. Not an ideal time to arrive at a summer seaside resort. Still, amid such gloom, a special aura pervaded St. Andrews-By-The-Sea.

St. Andrews is just across the Maine border in Canada's province of New Brunswick. Founded by United Loyalists in 1783, it is one of New Brunswick's oldest towns. Tree-lined streets shade authentic, rather than restored, mid-19th century homes set in spacious lawns.

Reeking with atmosphere, Shiretown Inn is Canada's first summer hotel. Located in the heart of town Shiretown remains a center of activity. As a rule, I dislike buffets, but ladeling homemade soup from an antique tureen and slicing fresh-from-the-oven bread, turned the usual tedium of serve-yourself lunch into a pleasure. Local specialties add to the menu. I especially enjoyed poached haddock and cinnamon-raisen toast for breakfast. After dinner you can join in an old-fashion sing-along around the piano or ask the waiter for crib and dart boards. Time has not caught up with St. Andrews-By-The-Sea.

Although a small town, St. Andrews boasts an unusual number of excellent accommodations. The most impressive hotel is the Algonquin, built by the Canadian-Pacific Railroad. This rambling Victorian hotel plays host to many conventions. A golf course, tennis courts, a swimming pool and other resort amenities make it popular year-round.

We stayed at Tara Manor. Rooms are spacious and attractive, some with adjoining sunrooms. All have private baths, rocking chairs, TVs and window boxes ablaze with begonias. Relaxing on Tara's 20 acres of park-like lawns and gardens is a vacation in itself. There is no dining room on the premises, but upon request Mrs. Ryall will serve breakfast in your room or on the patio overlooking the sea. Her husband cordially suggests good restaurants and side-trips.

Assuring me that the Rossmont Inn was a memorable place for dinner, Mr. Ryall phoned for reservations. Rossmont Inn, situated on an 87-acre estate embodies elegance in comfortable surroundings. Rooms are furnished with fine antiques from around the world. Hallways serve as bright, spacious sitting rooms for individual bedrooms. Home-cooked meals are served in the gracious tradition of another era; crystal and silver gleaming in the glow of candles and firelight. George and Marion Brewin are quite proud that former President Lyndon Johnson was a guest at their estate Inn.

Smaller inns and guest houses are scattered throughout the town. But wherever you stay, there is plenty to see and do in and around St. Andrews.

Due to its funnel shape, the Bay of Fundy produces the highest tides in the world. Market Wharf, across the square from Shiretown Inn, is a pleasant place to watch the tide's phenomenal rise and fall. Also a good spot from which to view the fishing boats bringing in their tremendous lobster catch.

At extreme low tide, nearby Minister's Island may be reached on foot or by car by way of a unique road "under the ocean." Tide tables are available at the local tourist bureau.

History buffs will enjoy the Charlotte County Historical Society (Water St.) containing furniture, desks, books, tools and unusual items all over 100 years old. You may also want to tour Block House, a unique restored fortification dating back to 1812.

For shoppers, Water Street, paralleling the shore, is chock-full of goodies. Shops featuring fine bone china and leather goods are interspersed with boutiques, antiques and handicrafts. Sea Captain's Loft sells everything from tartan kilts to Eskimo art. Handwoven items including blankets, suites, coats, hats, etc., are sold at St. Andrews Woolens Shop. Wool bought from local farmers is cleaned, dyed and spun into blends, then woven and tailored. Tweeds for skirts with matching yarn for sweaters makes a terrific gift. Samples of fabric and yarn may be obtained by writing St. Andrews Woolens Shop, P.O. Box 248, St. Andrews By-The-Sea, New Brunswick, Canada.

Sunbury Shores Arts and Nature Center is open during July and August. Workshops in painting, pottery, weaving, silver and natural science are offered. The center features programs, exhibitions, lectures and field trips.

For a field trip on your own, a visit to Huntsman Marine Laboratory and Aquarium will be enjoyable if life beneath the sea fascinates you. Maybe you prefer to catch rather than watch. Try deep-sea fishing aboard the "Bo-Peep" (daily except Saturday at 8:30 am and 2:00 pm). For fresh-water fishing, Chamcook Lake is teeming with trout and landlocked salmon.

Campobello and Deer Island are nearby. Long renowned as the summer home of the late President Franklin Roosevelt, Campobello remains unspoiled. Besides Roosevelt's "cottage" you can see Benedict Arnold's house at Snug Cove and places associated with the English Loyalist settlement. This tiny island has some isolated beaches and great rock formations. It is reached by a bridge from Lubec, Maine.

A ferry from Eastport, Maine takes you to Deer Island. Known as "Little Scotland of the Maritimes," this tiny island is famous for deep-sea fishing, lobster pounds and a whirlpool, "Old Sow," second in size only to Norway's Maelstrom.

While you are in the vicinity of St. Andrews By-The-Sea you really should take the auto ferry to Grand Manàn. For more about this excursion, read Yester Isle—Grand Manan, p.64.

Retreat
to a Hideaway
Getaway

V

COOLFONT–WHERE THE LIVIN' IS EASY

EMPHASIZING SPIRITUAL, AS WELL as the physical, Coolfont expresses a re-creative way-of-life. A well-rounded back-to-nature program is geared to tranquility, human understanding and recreation at your own pace. Located in the mountains of West Virginia, a few miles north of Berkley Springs, Coolfont is encircled by a pure mountain stream. Peace and quiet permeate the clear, fresh air.

Privacy is the keynote of this forested mountain retreat. Attractive A-frame chatlets (appropriately named Aspen, Luzerne, etc.) are tucked into the wooded hills at well-chosen sites. Invisible from the road, the cottages have views of mountains, lakes and trees. Each cabin has its own fireplace and fully equipped kitchen. Coolfont is open all year and in addition to rental chatlets, there is also a large campground where you can rent furnished tents.

For delicious food with companionship and some good conversation, you will enjoy the Treetop Restaurant and Squirrel's Nest in the main lodge. A huge stone fireplace in the lobby is a favorite gathering spot at the end of the day.

Riding, hiking and biking trails wind through miles of mountain woods and creek banks. No license is needed to fish in two beautiful lakes—one stocked with rainbow trout, the other teeming with a variety of fish. There's tennis, boating and lake swimming at a white sand beach. An 18-hole championship golf course is available about 10 minutes from Coolfont.

Special attractions are highlighted year-round. From May through

October, mountain mini-safaris and riverboat trips are popular. So are fish frys, hay rides and fireside forums. During the winter months snowshoe hiking, ice skating, ice fishing, sledding and cross-country skiing are among Coolfont's activities.

Located in a section rich in scenic beauty and historic significance, Coolfont is within easy reach of many places of interest: scenic drives, state parks, battlefields and caverns. Nearby Berkley Springs seems an unlikely town in which to find Roman Baths until you learn the original name was Ye Town of Bath. A tiny, picturesque park in the heart of town, frequently referred to as George Washington's bathtub, is the site of the oldest spa in America. Here warm mineral springs produce three million gallons of health-giving water daily. Undoubtedly, the baths are the biggest bargain I've encountered: the only service I know to bear the same price tag since 1967. Luxurious treatment includes a Roman bath, heat cabinet, shower and massage for only $5.00.

"The Castle" on a cliff overlooking Berkley Springs is an anachronism. Built by an aging Colonel for his youthful bride, this massive stone structure is an exact replica of the Barkley Castle in England. Tour its twenty rooms furnished with antiques and learn of its romantic history.

Arts and crafts are important at Coolfont. An art studio, appealing to both adults and children, offers exhibitions and instructions in candle making, decoupage, sandcasting, pottery, stained glass, quilting or almost anything. Come learn or come teach. Participation is a delightful innovation at Coolfont. Artists are welcome to stay here and share their talents.

The entertainment barn welcomes you too. Bring your own musical instrument, your voice or your dancing shoes. Join in the hootenannies, square dancing and folk-singing, or for a change of pace attend a lecture on Transcendental Meditation.

This may sound like a lot of action, but Coolfont has no organized regime—do your own thing, your own way, in your own time. There is plenty of space for solitude and serenity.

Exuding the relaxed, comfortable attitude of Coolfont, Sam Ashelman refers to his tastefully planned vacation spot as a "happy living experience." If your yen for the simple life is for a day, a week, or a lifetime, go to Coolfont—where the livin' is easy.

(Address: Coolfont, Berkley Springs, W.Va.
Phone: 304/258-1793.)

SPAS IN FLORIDA AND TEXAS
LEVITATING IN LUXURY

We HAVE EXPLORED GETAWAYS THAT combine leisure-time activities with inspiration and education. Now how about a retreat where you can be relaxed, refreshed and revitalized while losing weight at the same time.

Man, with all his scientific acumen, has never discovered a way to convert calories into curves (the right ones, anyway). It is possible, however, to lose avoirdupois with the proper combination of pampering and directed discipline combined with leisurely luxury in serene surroundings. If that sounds too good to be true, you haven't been to The Greenhouse, near Dallas, Texas.

For a richly rewarding experience, mentally as well as physically, I highly recommend a week (two if you can afford the time and money) at a beauty and health spa.

During a Sunday-to-Sunday program at The Greenhouse you experience, in a rarefied atmosphere, a new beneficial outlook and in-look. Every detail of decor and service is geared to luxury, leisure and loveliness. Rooms are spacious, decorated in subtle, soothing shades.

But let me just outline a typical week. Arrival time is Sunday afternoon. After unpacking and exploring your accommodations, noting the sunken tub with an array of complimentary cosmetics and a welcoming letter with a Neiman-Marcus credit card, tea is served. In a gardened patio around a sky-vaulted pool, you meet your fellow guests.

A sumptuous 400-calorie dinner (oh, yes it is) is served in a charming dining room. A new color scheme of flowers, china, crystal, silver and linens each evening is enough to take your mind off any lingering hunger pangs. Actually, tiny portions are so deftly served, that by slowly savoring each course (and partaking heartily of the parsley) you feel quite satisfied. Demitasse follows in the golden drawing room. Entertainment is omitted on Sunday nights to allow time for a doctor and nurse to give you a going over and discuss the weekly regimen.

Monday morning at 8:00 am you are awakened with a breakfast tray, your shades drawn and bath run. Now I've never really been a breakfast in bed fancier, but believe me, under these conditions, I could easily become addicted. Fresh flowers in a cut-glass vase, butterfly china, delicate linens, the rich aroma of coffee—why you feel as though the Texas egg and melba toast is a banquet. Your daily schedule makes exciting reading:

8:00	Breakfast in bed
8:30	Wake-up exercise—around indoor pool
9:00	Swing and sway the Greenhouse way—outdoor pool
10:00	Sauna and needle shower
10:15	Massage
11:00	Water exercise
12:00	Beauty school
1:00	Luncheon
2:00	Facial
3:00	Spot reducing and individual instruction
3:30	Hair treatment and styling
4:00	Manicure and pedicure
6:00	Coctails (?) in drawing room followed by dinner
8:00	Entertainment

94

Everyone dons identical costumes—blue leotards and yellow rose of Texas terrycloth robes. Classes are divided into small groups for maximum individual attention. All treatment rooms are blissfully quiet. A friendly, competent staff of specialized experts outnumber guests 65 to 36. With such personal pampering interspersed with morning boullion and afternoon juice breaks, you hardly realize any aches and pains from all these accelerated gymnastics.

Evening entertainment includes a variety of "psyche-stimulating" diversions. You might see a glamorous fashion or jewelry show from Neiman-Marcus, join in a discussion on wines or dreams, or receive instruction in dance or yoga. Frequently Helen Corbitt, the culinary wizard responsible for the fabulous cuisine at The Greenhouse, talks on food and a once-a-week trip to Neiman-Marcus is planned.

Some of the women wear evening attire, others prefer a rest from dress-up and make-up. You can do your own thing and move at your own pace, even taking all your meals in your room if you seek complete solitude. It is not necessary to leave the building to follow the entire beauty program. To be so secluded from every day hustle and bustle, so ensconced in harmonious surroundings, concentrating on improving the way you look, feel, dress and even the way you think is a spirit-lifting total experience.

For those who prefer their beauty and health program à la co-ed, Palm Aire in Pompano Beach, Florida, is the place. Situated in a luxurious, tropical setting, Palm Aire encompasses a way of life devoted to the concept of the "good life through good health, vigor, a tranquil mind and trim body."

Your visit begins with an examination by a resident physician. Then your day's activities and daily calories are carefully planned to give you a balanced diet, hydro-therapy and exercise program.

Exercise in classrooms and outdoor pools, jog along the beach, golf on one of five courses, or play tennis. Relax in the sauna, siesta room, or in the lush garden setting of the Spa's Roman baths. Have a massage or whirlpool bath in outdoor privacy.

How about something really different? An herbal wrap! This ancient Egyptian custom consists of wrapping the body in unbleached linen sheets which have been steamed in a specially formulated herbal solution. Although relaxation of body and spirit is its primary purpose, it does help draw out excess fluids.

For the ultimate in pampering, you can't beat a Loofa bath. Your body is cleansed with a special salt and oil treatment, then scrubbed with natural loofa and pure soap to loosen dead cells, and rinsed away with an invigorating Scotch spray. Your skin glows and has the texture of a baby's.

Food is necessarily not the high point at Palm Aire. But you will really enjoy the dietic meals, hardly realizing you are consuming only six or eight hundred calories a day. Bright, spacious rooms have two queen-sized beds, two dressing rooms and two complete baths, and a balcony or terrace overlying a fairway or gardens.

Evenings at the spa are up to you—from bridge in your room, backgammon in the game room, dancing and entertainment in Palm Aire's clubhouse, to jai alai next door and doing the town (Miami, Fort Lauderdale, Pompano and Palm Beach).

A week or two at any first-rate spa does cost a lot of money, but the benefits are far more than most vacations. You can gain a new lease on life. And best of all, you can lose weight while levitating in luxury.

THE DOOR PENINSULA—ONE KEY TO TRANQUILITY

"NORTH OF THE TENSION LINE" is a phrase sometimes used to describe Washington Island, northernmost tip of Wisconsin's Door Peninsula. I think this subtle allusion to mental readjustment is one key to the Peninsula's popularity. Bisecting Lake Michigan and Green Bay, in the shape of an exclamation mark, the Door Peninsula combines unspoiled wilderness with just the right amount of acculturation. Its 40 miles of rugged coastal shores, tranquil bays, cherry orchards and unique villages are fanned by natural breezes from each direction. A draw-bridge over a busy canal at Sturgeon Bay is the only access to this scenic, uncluttered isle with its overtones of Scandinavia.

Lake Michigan's shoreline is densely forested, with only a few hamlets dotting its coast. Several picturesque towns tucked into Green Bay's shore each reflect a distinct personality, but all exude an indefinable quality of refreshing quiescence.

It's no wonder Jens Jensen, landscape architect and philosopher, discovered here the true significance of nature and life. Jensen chose Ellison Bay, once an Indian village, for his unique retreat, The Clearing. He invited everyone to share with him this "atmosphere where man could clear his mind in a woodland setting rich in nature's simple lesson." Since Jensen's death in 1951, the Wisconsin Farm Bureau, an independent organization of farm families, has maintained The Clearing for business and professional men and women, artists and teachers, young or old, who desire quietude and inspiration. Classes and seminars are offered on art, music, literature, philosophy, natural science and crafts. Study assumes a new dimension in these peaceful, forested corridors.

Hidden in cathedral-like woods, The Clearing comprises dormitories, an old school house and a charming ivy-covered stone lodge with a dining room library, lobby and teachers' rooms. A schedule of weekly seminars, including prices, etc., as well as a new book, *The Story of the Clearing*, can be ordered from The Clearing, Ellison Bay, Wisc. 54210.

For campers who love to get back to nature and rough it, five parks in this region boast hundreds of campsites throughout acres of wooded terrain and 20 miles of roads. For the more luxury oriented, there is an array of motels ranging from large resorts to small cabins. Early reservations are essential in the summer. Skiing and snowmobiling are making this an increasingly popular winter-time vacation spot. Spring blossoms and autumnal grandeur lure the nature-loving segment.

Ephraim, founded in 1853 by Moravians, is located in the center of the Door Peninsula. Emitting an old-world charm with white church spires and rambling verandahs with rocking chairs, this picturesque town reveres its religious heritage. The Edgewater Motel offers an unparalleled view of Ephraim's famed sunsets.

Many outstanding restaurants offer innovative menus and intriguing decor. One eye-stopper in the heart of Sister Bay is Al Johnson's Swedish Restaurant. We've heard of bats in the belfry—but would you believe goats on a grass roof? Sure enough, playing and grazing on the sod roof of an authentic Sweedish log chatlet are two frisky goats. Breakfast is served all day and cold fruit soup, usually served as an appetizer, becomes a yummy desert with a scoop of vanilla ice cream.

"Fish boils" are peculiarly indigenous to this region. Originating over a hundred years ago, this simple way to prepare a meal has become a legend. A festive air and aroma accompany the seafood dinner boiled in a large kettle over an open fire. The head "boiler" heaps two chunks of "17 minute" boiled fish with potatoes and onions on a plate which you carry to a long table. Generous portions of cole slaw, pickles, fresh bread, cherry pie and "conversation" complete the ceremony.

Fish Creek probably sees more action than all the other villages. Even so, the overtones are cultural rather than commercial. The annual Peninsula Music Festival takes place here each August. Throughout the summer, "Theatre in a Garden" is the stage for plays presented by the oldest professional residential summer stock company in America. Many artists and craftsmen have chosen Fish Creek as the setting for their creativity.

Hugging the shores of Lake Michigan, near Bailey's Harbor, Ridges Sanctuary is one of the nation's largest corporately-owned wildflower sanctuaries. Many of the rare plants are sub-Arctic species deposited during the glacial period. A variety of birds and wildlife can be glimpsed from the biking and hiking trails lacing the ridges. Also of interest are "range lights," built in 1870 to guide ships safely through the reefs.

I would plan my next visit to Bailey's Harbor to include a Wednesday. That's the day the chapel at "Bjorklunden Vid Sjan" (Birch Forest by the Water) is open. The remarkable history of this special chapel is one of faith. Winifred Boynton reacted creatively to the numerous sorrows of her life. After becoming totally deaf, thus ending her career as a concert pianist, she studied art and architecture. Following the tragic death of her first husband, Winifred fulfilled her dream of building a chapel dedicated to peace within, thence peace throughout the world. It took nine years to build their family sanctuary of peace. Each intricate detail was handcarved with love and dedication. Today it

99

inspires all who step within its joyous stillness.

Tourism, fishing and boating may be the economic mainstay of the Door Peninsula. Just as essential, however, to its continuing growth and character is the intrinsic key—tranquility.

MICHIGAN STATE UNIVERSITY
GETAWAY WITH HEIGHTENED HORIZONS

PROFESSORS LEAVE THE CAMPUS to take sabbaticals from their academic schedules. How about a reverse twist? Did it ever occur to you that a sabbatical from your daily routine spent *on a campus* could be richly rewarding?

Michigan State University in East Lansing is an idyllic place to stimulate your artistic, emotional and educational interests while enjoying a leisurely vacation. Continuing education is not a new idea. Thoreau urged, one hundred years ago, that we not abandon education with graduation, rather, "pursue liberal studies the rest of our lives."

On a luscious summer evening while strolling through the gardens accompanied by the playful sounds of birds and carillon chimes, Thoreau's idea hit. Here was an unusual getaway, a hide-away retreat amidst uncluttered beauty, tranquility and leisure-time activities with educational opportunities galore—a getaway with heightened horizons. Can you do it if you're over 40, 50, 60? Yes, you can. Let me tell you.

Whether you want to enroll in classes for credit, start a new career, schedule a similar-interest conference or merely absorb a rarefied atmosphere in beautiful surroundings, you will be delighted with Michigan State.

More than 15,000 trees and shrubs, and over 5000 plant species transform a college campus into an arboretum park. Plantings landscaped with an understated naturalness. Walks, flower-bordered pathways and a shaded ribbon of river wind through one of the nation's largest, most beautiful campuses.

101

Michigan State University, founded in 1855, was America's first agricultural land grant college. Sixty-three students and three buildings have grown into over 40,000 students enrolled in 17 separate colleges, comprising 400 buildings on 5000 acres. The multi-dimensional continuing education program enables thousands more to tap resources of one of the world's leading universities. Educational pursuits vary according to individual aspirations. But the University's buildings, recreational facilities and many attractions can be enjoyed by all, young, middle-aged and elderly.

The Kellogg Center for Continuing Education is the campus guest house and conference center. All its modern rooms are air-conditioned, spacious and have color TV. The State Room is an elegant dining room serving traditional meals. Well-equipped conference facilities in this seven-story building are in continuous use throughout the year.

A calendar of events can be obtained by writing the Department of Information Services, 109 Agriculture Hall, MSU, East Lansing, Mich. In addition to special programs, concerts, seminars and exhibitions, monthly conferences are listed. One month's schedule might include such diversified programs as a figure skating clinic, International Council of Shopping Centers or transportation for the elderly and handicapped. What are your interests? Urban development, human ecology, criminal justice? You name it. The faculty at MSU is ready, willing and able to assist and enlighten at an educational meeting of your choice.

Beaumont Tower, the campus landmark, stands on the site of the first building in America erected for the teaching of scientific agriculture. Bronze bells from the tower's carillon awaken students each morning at 7:50 and herald twilight at 5:00. Concerts every Sunday afternoon and many during summer evenings are always popular.

102

Galleries in the Kresge Art Center (a Gift of the Kresge Foundation) serve as a teaching laboratory as well as a treasure house for important art exhibits. A modern library contains more than 2,000,000 volumes.

From a 500,000 year-old mammoth to a frontier trading post, you can view displays of civilization's emergence in the three floors of the MSU Museum. Dioramas of Indian lore and native wildlife are highlights in the exhibits portraying Michigan history. You can find unusual imported items for sale in the gift shop.

Abrams Planetarium is one of the most active in the world, both in equipment and programming. Dramatic productions with special audio and visual effects are presented in its 254-seat sky theater. A highly advanced star projector is housed here.

A small brick interfaith chapel was built in 1952 to memorailize MSU students who gave their lives while defending their country. Assorted stones from several ancient European cathedrals are set in the chapel's walls.

Plans are underway for a $16 million dollar center for the performing arts. The complex will include a 600-seat theater, a laboratory theater and a 2500-seat great hall with acoustical columns to enhance symphony, opera and ballet. Until its completion, outstanding dramatic and musical productions are presented in the Auditorium which seats 3000.

Leisure time activities are not limited to culture. You can skate year-round at one or two large ice-skating arenas. For golfers there's an 18-hole championship course, as well as a 9-hole course, driving range and practice greens. Forty surfaced tennis courts, two swimming pools, a bowling alley and an activity room for gymnastics and dancing round out an extensive sports facility.

Quiet places abound through 96 miles of walkways and 12 miles of bicycle paths. Red Cedar River, traversing the Northern 2000 acres of the campus, is a perfect setting for canoes and rowboats. Many off-campus restaurants offer tempting food in unusual surroundings. The Depot, originally a train station, follows the railroad theme from its oversized baggage claim menu to a baggage car salad bar.

Machus Red Fox on the other hand is as sophisticated an eatery as you'll find in any large city. Beggar's Banquet is so exceptional I have one friend who frequently drives a hundred miles to eat there. I really think she is as fascinated with Noah's Ark, a pet shop close by, as she is with the restaurant. You can find unusual animals, but the owners get so attached to them they just may refuse to sell you that exciting boa constrictor you can't live without.

Interesting nearby side-trips from the campus include the State capital in Lansing. Until 1847, Detroit was the capital, but fearing the border city might be invaded, the legislature decided to move. After many months of debate as to where the new seat of government was to locate, someone (in jest) suggested Lansing. Lacking a better solution, the capital was moved to an isolated area which consisted of a log house and sawmill. Today the skyline includes, along with a beautiful capital dome, many modern government buildings, church steeples and the 25-story Olds Tower—now called the Michigan National Tower.

Driving South from Lansing to the Irish Hills takes you through typical small towns with tree-canopied streets, village greens and clock towers. Small, sparkling lakes dot the unspoiled countryside which many say looks just like Ireland.

To the West you'll find Holland, which makes the most of its name with a windmill, a wooden shoe factory, Dutch Village, Netherlands Museum and masses of colorful tulips.

To find a bit of Bavaria, go Northeast to Frankenmuth. This German community is noted throughout the state for old-world chicken dinners served at the Bavarian Inn and at Zehnder's. Bronner's, a year-round Christmas shop, is another drawing card, along with the town's yearly Bavarian Festival in June.

I hope this portrayal of activities and attractions on and around a university campus have added a provocative dimension to your vacation plans. Alone or in a group, you can make your leisure time more productive—plan a getaway with heightened horizons and fun.

SWANNANOA—TERRACES OF THE MIND

INSPIRATION, SERENITY AND SPIRIT at Swannanoa are beyond words. Situated atop Afton Mountain, near Waynesboro, Virginia, is an unbelievable shrine of beauty. Feeding the soul as well as the senses, this Italian Renaissance palace with its terraced sculpture gardens commands a breathtaking view of the Shenadoah Valley and the Blue Ridge Mountains of Virginia.

The romantic story behind Swannanoa is a fairy tale come true. Dr. Walter Russell and his beautiful wife, Lao, discovered in their love for each other, for man, and for God, a way of life they dedicated their lives to sharing with the world.

Internationally renowned as one of the most versatile men in America, Walter Russell achieved greatness as a sculptur, painter, architect, composer, author, philosopher, and Doctor of Science. Lao Russell, too, is equally accomplished.

Lao had a dream. She saw Christ illuminating the world from a high pinnacle. His message was Brotherly Love and the unity of man with man and with God. Her soul's desire was to find a sacred mountain; to fill it with inspired writings, paintings, sculpture and other works of art and science; to create a shrine of beauty to illumine the heart and soul of mankind throughout the ages.

Together these two kindred-kind searched the United States for this sacred mountain. They found it in the Blue Ridge Mountains of the South. Together they transformed a ruined marble palace in a jungle into a glorious mountain paradise.

Their teachings are known as "The Science of Spiritual Man". Swannanoa is called The University of Science and Philosophy. More than just a place to see, it is a way-of-life to inspire one to greater and more creative living.

"The Divine Illiad," "The Secret of Light," "The Man Who Tapped the Secrets of the Universe," and "God Will Work With You But Not For You" are a few of their inspiring books. A joint-authored one-year Home Study Course in Universal Law, Natural Science and Philosophy has spread throughout the world their teachings of the Light within man.

These noted works on philosophy and science are housed in the magnificient palace constructed of Georgia marble on the outside and Italian marble on the inside. Light floods through a spectacular Tiffany stained glass window at the top of a marble double staircase, with hand-painted domed ceiling above.

It reportedly took 300 master artisans eight years to build this handsome structure in 1912. The estimated cost of building it today would be twenty million dollars. Huge rooms with rare wood carvings and mural paintings are full of the great collection of the Russels' masterpieces in all the arts.

Theodore Roosevelt, Franklin D. Roosevelt, Thomas Edison, Charles Goodyear and General Douglas MacArthur are a few of the Great Americans Walter Russel memorialized in stone. Few other sculptors have created such expressive eyes. He seems to capture the very light of their souls.

Amazing in scope and detail is his Mark Twain Memorial. Mark Twain is seated in the center of all 28 characters from his books. The Four Freedoms Monument, created at President Roosevelt's request, depicts Freedom of Speech, Freedom of Religion, Freedom from Want and Freedom from Fear. Four angels in human form, two men and two women, with their wings upraised, face the four points of the compass. Glen Clark declared this dramatic sculpture

107

to be our symbol of Freedom to the world.

Highlighting his collection of paintings is "The Might of Ages." This noble painting, symbolizing the power of thought in the building of civilization, received high honors and awards from eleven foreign countries.

Seldom in history have so many of the works and memorabilia of one genius been housed in one place during his lifetime. Scrapbooks containing newspaper and magazine articles describe his scientific discoveries and the twenty million dollars worth of buildings he planned and built. Autographs and personal letters bear the signatures of the world's great, such as Caruso, Paderewski, Theodore Roosevelt, Rudyard Kipling, George Bernard Shaw, Cordull Hull, and King Albert of Belgium.

Dominating the terraced gardens with their majestic trees and rose covered pergola is the towering, compassionate Christ of The Blue Ridge, envisaged by Lao and sculpted in collaboration with her husband. A sense of tranquility permeates the gardens and meditation is enhanced by strains of old world music reverberating through the poetic shadows.

If your heart's desire is an uplifting experience of meditation or if you are just looking for a palace full of art treasures and beautiful gardens, you should plan a trip to Western Virginia. Twenty five miles from Charlottesville, eleven miles from Staunton and four miles from Waynesboro, Swannanoa is a tangible tribute to the intangible forces which generate the peace and happiness for which all men yearn.

Open year round. Summer 8 a.m. to dusk. Winter 9 a.m. to 5 p.m. Admission to Palace and Gardens $1, children 50¢. Admission to Gardens only 50¢. Holiday Inn with fabulous view located 1 mile away. Interstate 64 and Route 250 at junction of Skyline Drive and Blue Ridge Parkway.

Room to Roam

VI

EARLY FALL IS AN IDEAL TIME to appreciate the beautiful whites of Maine—fleecy clouds, frothy surf, tender birches, clapboard houses and church steeples. Tourists in search of white sand and white sails have gone home. It is not yet time for crowds in search of white snow, so the serenity, quiescence and beauty of Maine are yours to explore.

Bar Harbor can be reached in three hours from Portland. But taking three days is much more fun. We decided to take our time and explore some of the towns along the way.

An easy 30-minute drive from Portland brings you to Yarmouth. You'll find the charming Homewood Inn. My first impression was one of striking contrasts: the summer sounds of water gently lapping against the rocks and the autumn smell of wood burning in the cottage fireplaces.

A fire was blazing in the "Abenaki Cellar," a unique cocktail lounge dug out of the old cellar space. We entered through original slanted cellar doors festively canopied in red. Over martinis, we scanned the menu, but not for long. "When in Maine"—what else? Lobster! Having heard about Maine Lobster all my life, I still wasn't prepared for the vast availability. At every turn, instead of a beef joint or pizza parlor, there was a lobster pound. We tried it every way—broiled, boiled, baked, sauteed, and stewed. Well, here at the Inn we were off to a great start. We revelled as we dipped each morsel in succulent drawn butter. Ummm!

110

Saturday dawned crisp and clear. Luxury of luxuries—no deadlines, no pressures, and no phone calls. Time to mosey around and stop wherever something piqued our fancy. A flea market was the first stop. It's fun to poke around eclectic "junk," buying something you nostalgically remember from childhood. But quite a jolt when you realize these items are now antiques! Time marches on and so did we, stopping at a large trading post where we outfitted ourselves in moccasins. We marvelled at our luck in stumbling onto such a find, not realizing these "second" shoe outlets were in every hamlet along the way. It was good timing though, since now shod in comfortable foot gear we were prepared for our next excursion. This proved to be the last thing we were expecting to find in Maine—a desert.

Yes, three miles off main highway (Route 95) and only 12 miles from the open sea near Freeport is the Desert of Maine. This natural phenomenon has been unearthed within recent times and is exactly what its name implies. We strolled over the sheerest of powdery sand and listened to a young lad relate the amazing history of its growth. At one time this area was a fertile farm. Gradually a tiny patch of sand appeared, slowly began to spread and continues even today. The sand assumes over one hundred different shades and tints. These are effectively arranged in sand "jars" of various shapes and sizes, forming artistic patterns and designs.

Leaving the unexpected sand dunes, we discovered a sprawling oasis at the top of Bailey Island. Cook's Lobster House, jutting out over the water, proved the very best lobster value we encountered anyplace. The pictorial "crib-stone" bridge between Bailey and Orr's Island is the only one of its kind in the country. A unique open stone lattice work allows the tides to rise and fall freely with no resistance.

On to Boothbay Harbor which has to be one of the most beautiful of the myriad harbors. This is what Maine is all about: rocky shorelines, boats, lighthouses, quaint shops and the rugged sea. Here, as throughout Maine, neatness prevails. Gardens, yards and even the streets are clean and tidy, an uncluttered frame for the glistening white houses with their imaginative variety of colored trim. Painters must have a heyday in Maine. Nowhere has paint been used with better taste.

Spruce Point Inn commands a spectacular view of the outer harbor. We enjoyed the sunset on a calm, peaceful sea. Sunrise found the mirror-smooth water transformed into turbulent, seething surf. We drove a few miles east to see one of the most photographed lighthouses in America. A stormy sea is an especially impressive background for a first glimpse of Pemaguid Point Lighthouse. We could almost feel the screeching North Easters that have battered this peninsula through the years. Sharing this magnificent jagged rock formation with hundreds of seagulls was an experience to remember.

History was brought even more vividly to life as we toured Pemaquid Peninsula. At the site of Fort William Henry, built in 1692, archeologists are unearthing relics of early days in the ruins of 16th and 17th century Indian settlements. Restoration plans are well underway.

The Clarissa Illsley Tavern in Damariscotta at the northern end of the peninsula is a gem of a restaurant. We were so impressed with the gracious atmosphere, the unusual decor in subtle shades of moss green and chocolate brown and the handsome pieces of authentic Early American furniture, that the food was incidental. The cuisine proved as distinctive as the surroundings, so study your map carefully and plan some meal here, no matter what.

Camden is a picture-book village. No wonder it has been described as the prettiest of all the pretty towns. Colorful baskets hang from every lamp-post. Schooner sails dot the seascape. Motels at each curve of the road compete for the most perfect view.

The Lobster Pound at Lincolnsville proved a real treat. Here we ordered our lobster in a stew. It was tasty, hearty and chock-full of lobster. But it was the home-made date pie that really caught my fancy. Richard McLaughlin happily shared his own personal recipe with me. Sounds so simple, but is so elegant.

2 cups dates
2 cups water
1 cup brown sugar
Pinch of salt

Cook until thick in heavy pot. Pile into prebaked pie shell and top with whipped cream.

While we were still licking our lips, he ran back to remind us that he used sharp dates from Iraq in this special recipe. No provincial town, this Lincolnsville.

Each village and each harbor has its own special charm. Ocean Drive, in Bar Harbor, is a winding, scenic feast. A jewel of a town, Bar Harbor is nestled in a curve on the shore.

The 180° panorama from our balcony at the Wonderview Motel was breathtaking. At close range we observed the grotesque, open habit of the pines as opposed to the closeknit symmetry of the blue spruce. Behind us rose craggy, pink coral cliffs jutting up to Cadillac Mountain, the highest point on the East Coast, north of Rio de Janeiro. This is the first spot to admit the rays of the sun as it soars above the rim of the world. As we turned our gaze out to sea, we could almost glimpse the very top of the world. Quite a lofty spot on which to end our brief holiday. Not enough time to have captured all the magic of Maine, but enough to know we want to return and meander more in Maine.

WHAT MAKES VERMONT SO SPECIALLY different? I foraged through miles of Vermont's natural beauty during foliage and discovered several reasons.

Foilage in Vermont is as definite a season as summer or Christmas. In Woodstock the peak of color brings the peak of leaf watchers. All of its charming Inns are filled and many private homes take in travelers. Their system for finding you a bed is unique. In a tiny booth on the village square a friendly man (from the Chamber of Commerce) notes your specific needs, makes a few phone calls, then directs you to lodgings, even suggesting a good restaurant or two.

I got over my disappointment of not staying at the Woodstock Inn when I met the McCormacks. Their home sits high atop Barberry Hill with a commanding view of Woodstock. The town's four church steeples with Paul Revere bells can be seen from this lofty site.

Woodstock is full of surprises. A covered bridge across from the oblong village green and the "town crier" blackboard under a clump of white birches smack of a past era. Handsomely preserved homes dating from the 1700's and 1800's grace the common. Galleries and shops line wide, tree-shaded streets.

F. H. Gillingham is a unique store. Since 1886, its old planked floors have been receiving customers in search of hardware, fresh poultry, dry goods or spirits. For a fascinating cocktail lounge and restaurant, visit the Rumble Seat. Walls papered with pages from old Saturday Evening Posts, copper antiques and an atmosphere of the Roaring 20's convert this subterranean rathskeller into a gem. Another must is the Woodstock Inn. From the warmth of old-timey quilts and white birch logs burning in fireplaces to the coolness of its Garden Terrace, Woodstock exudes traditional Vermont charm.

But back to the McCormack's. Dave had just returned from a Citizen's meeting where the topic under discussion was a proposed hi-rise condominium. While listening to him tell of negative reactions to the new building and eating some of his wife's excellent cherry pie, I learned quite a bit about Vermonters. They revere independence—both political and individual. In fact, what many mistakenly take for their austere disinterest is in reality a respect for a personal life-style of live and let live.

The constitution adopted in Vermont after the signing of the Declaration of Independence was the first in the nation to outlaw slavery and to establish universal voting privileges without property considerations. "Preserving this land" and protecting Vermont's natural beauty are tantamount to biblical commandments. To this day Vermonters deeply resent and fight any attempted increase in federal controls and any infringement of the state motto—Freedom and Unity.

Weston is a short, scenic drive from Woodstock along Echo Lake. A typical Vermont village, its Main Street is lined with quaint shops on both sides of the Village Green. The Vermont Country Store and Restaurant are a real find. Built in 1820 as a residence, the restaurant oozes nostalgic allure. You can enjoy good food in one of several Victorian dining rooms or in an authentic 1885 barroom. Its magnificent mahogany bar, rich paneling, back mirrors and touches of gold create a cozy but elegant atmosphere.

The Country Store next door is as "general" as you can get. Sleigh bells, ice cream freezers, overalls, red flannels, and licorice—black, red, green or by the yard. And the men playing checkers around an old pot-bellied stove complete the picture.

Down the street at Ellie Ballow's, an old wood stove is the piece de resistance. Your husband can warm his hands while you try on the latest in overall dresses. Vermont's oldest summer theater is located in Weston. So is the unusual Bowl Mill. Here you can watch all sorts of wooden products being made. Active since 1902, the old mill and annex abound with an unbelievable collection of Vermont-made woodenware.

Over the hill in the hamlet of Landgrove, you'll find a real country Inn. They offer not only pleasant accommodations, but "great vittles."

Vermont's back roads are a far cry from teeming turnpikes. A rippling stream curves along nearly every mile. No cluttering signs or billboards mar the multi-colored tapestries of hillside forests, white birches and mountain brooks.

Just as Vermont's old-world villages share much in common—neat homes with well-kept lawns and flower gardens, marvelous inns, flavorful shops, and quaint churches—so they each have something inherently individual.

In Middleburg you must not miss the Bakery Lane Soup Bowl. Tucked midway down tiny Bakery Lane on the banks of Otter Creek, this unique restaurant serves homemade soups, breads, salads and desserts. Another house specialty is hot mulled wine. Food and atmosphere are great!

Grafton is a lived-in town, restored to its original charm. The Old Tavern has been a popular Inn since 1801. Gallery North Star is brand new and well worth a visit. In a remarkable atelier, Mel and Nancy Hunter invite you to watch the complex processes involved in producing lithographs, etchings and engravings. Of course, you are also welcome to browse around and view their handsome collection of paintings and sculpture. Covered Bridge Cheddar Cheese is a fun place just a "whoop and holler" from the Gallery. You will enjoy both a covered bridge and cheese plant and sample as well as watch the cheese being made.

Among Manchester's numerous attractions I found two exceptional shops. For the ultimate in the unusual be sure to visit Jelly Mill and Jelly Mill Too. Really extraordinary, quality furniture, clothing, jewelry and gift items from all over the world are sold in an old dairy barn and new annex. Whether you shop for something unique or lunch on the balcony overlooking ponds and mountains, you will revel in the "experience" of the Jelly Mill.

The Enchanted Doll House has seven rooms chock full of whimsey. Dolls of every sort, imaginative toys and miniatures of everything in the world. Browse, buy or settle down with their extensive catalog. Collector or not, you will be spellbound with the fantastic selection of doll house furniture and accessories. If you don't have children or grandchildren of your own, you'll just have to get a teddy bear or something for yourself in this land of make-believe.

Well, you see I found a few reasons why Vermont is special and different. Leisurely pace, enchanting villages, intriguing shops, charming Inns, solitude, quiet and technicolor reflections in sparkling lakes. I'm sure you will uncover several good ones of your own when you go foraging and foliaging in Vermont.

NORTHWEST MONTANA–CORNUCOPIA FOR CAMPERS

MORE AND MORE PEOPLE are taking to the hills—with backpacks, tents and campers. Well, all you nature lovers are in for a treat. Get out your Atlas, look Northwest and start thinking big. Montana's slogan, "Land of the Big Skys," could refer equally to its big mountains, plains, wilderness, wildlife, waters, parks, even to its hats—Montana is just plain big!

In no area of our great country have I been more enthralled with the farming panorama. A patchwork quilt of wheat fields interspersed with acres of fallow land form a massive rural mosaic. Cattle graze in lush green meadows, feathered by rivulets and springs. Towns are few and far between, leaving vast areas of unspoiled natural beauty uncluttered and unchanged.

Route 89 from Great Falls to Glacier National Park must have been the inspiration for the song, "On a clear day, you can see forever." Reaching out to the decks of your vision is a limitless green table-land of grazing farm country rimmed by smoky blue mountains. Cloud patterns configurate the green landscape and it is hard to distinguish clouds from snow peaks merging in the distance.

Glacier National Park is a glorious wonderland of scenic delights. Snow-crested mountains cradle shimmering lakes. Water crashes through deep gorges, cascades along narrow rifts and tumbles into rock-bedded streams. Evergreen forests and tranquil wildflower meadows contrast sharply with jagged, rocky peaks and ice-carved glaciers. Geologically dating back a half-billion years

118

or so, its million acres of spectacular primitive wilderness provides a cornucopia for campers and nature lovers.

Camp sites are more plentiful than resort accommodations. Several of Glacier's campgrounds have paved road access with trailer space. Many more lie along gravel roads that permit tents only. Visitor information centers and range stations can acquaint you with guided walks, campfire programs and the park's numerous resources, activities and amazing geological history.

Throughout a thousand miles of well-marked trails, you might catch sight of deer, elk, bears and mountain goats. Bicycling can be fun in certain areas. Horse trips are operated out of others. Boating is permitted on Glacier's lakes and no license is required to fish in the park's 200 lakes and streams. Ski-touring and snow-shoeing are becoming increasingly popular.

For the less adventurous visitor, the park operates seven Chalet Hotels. Situated at the most scenic points throughout the park, these handsome Alpine-type resorts are constructed of native timber. Massive columns in magnificent lobbies are made from 800-year-old Douglas fir trees. For hotel reservations, call toll free 800/332-4114.

Camping facilities in Montana's wide-open spaces are not confined to state parks. Flathead Lake, the largest fresh water lake West of the Mississippi, lies in the shadows of the towering glaciers. Miles of cherry orchards extend along its banks. Snugly ensconced on the South shore of Flathead, the town of Polson is far removed from tourists, yet pulsating with activities campers care about.

Fishing probably ranks first. Montana boasts the best trout fishing in the world (and also brags about bass and perch). Well, the big pond in Polson's front yard has to be home for some of them. Pick up a copy of Montana fishing regulations and a map at a sporting goods store before wetting your line, so you'll know where, when and how.

Sailing is also good on Flathead. Sailboat rentals are available at Bear Harbor and Inland Charter on the West shore. Two-hour excursions on "Retta-Mary" are scheduled twice daily. The 8:00 pm cruise is a terrific way to watch the sun set behind the mountains.

A golf course on the shores of the lake looks challenging. Horseback riding and bicycling are popular and for veterate shoppers there are many antique shops. The Village Shop on Route 93 East of Polson has an unusual collection of antique telephones (more than 300 at last count). One of the largest bottle collections in the world and ancient Roman coins can be found at Tiny's Tavern (7 miles North of the Bison Range). For more up-to-date items, stop at The Montana Copper Shop on Main Street in Polson. Anything that can possibly be made from or trimmed with copper is there.

A great place for breakfast is right across the street. Price's Good Food isn't a very original name for a restaurant, but the price is right and the food is good. Try the house specialty—Texas toast. Pieces of thick bread are grilled and served with honey.

Polson's interesting history is captured and brought to life at the Polson Museum. Its Fiddlers Hall of Fame was probably inspired by the town's namesake, David Polson, who ranged his herds here in 1870. He used to strap a fiddle on his back and ride horseback to play for country dances and Indian pow-wows.

Maybe you'll luck into a colorful pow-wow at the nearby Flathead Reservation. There is square dancing the second Saturday of July and August. The Montana Fiddler Championship takes place in Polson each summer.

Moving into the foothills, 18,000 acres of valley grassland and forested areas are devoted to a big game sanctuary. The National Bison Range shelters herds of deer, elk, big horn sheep, antelope and mountain goats. Keep your eyes peeled throughout a 19-mile drive, for there is no telling what you'll see, maybe some of the 100,000 soaring waterfowl that nest in reservoirs and water holes of the nearby Ninepipe and Pablo National Wildlife Refuge.

Another point of interest in Flathead Valley is St. Ignatius Mission, established by Jesuits in 1854. Located in a small village of the same name, the mission stands as a living and beautiful memorial to the Jesuits' endeavor to share Christianity with the Indians during their catastrophic struggles. Colorful paintings and murals adorn the walls and ceilings. Soft Gregorian chants resound throughout the sanctuary—an unexpected oasis of tranquility in the "land of big skys."

VICTORIA AND VANCOUVER
A VERITABLE FERRYLAND

FOR SOME STRANGE REASON, I tend to believe nearly everything I read and almost everything I hear. If a restaurant sounds great, I try it. When a city is described as fascinating, I go. Where scenery is painted as spectacular, I have to see it. Somewhere I read that if there is something new under the sun, you'll find it in British Columbia. Five days later, I was there!

Snow-capped mountains aren't new, nor are lush, fertile meadows. Sparkling mountain lakes aren't new, neither are wooded islands. Even glaciers, fjords and totem poles, though scarce, aren't new. All of these in dramatic profusion, superimposed in one panoramic kaliedoscope—that's new! That's British Columbia.

Whether blue, green, turquoise, even when grey, you won't find the sea more dazzling than in the cool waterways, inlets and coves embracing Victoria and Vancouver. "Princess Marguerite," a modern ferry almost the size of an ocean liner, sails from the Seattle Wharf at 8:30 a.m. each morning. Four hours later you dock at the picturesque inner harbor of Victoria. This water entrance to the capital of British Columbia is literally a doorstep to the stately, ivy-covered Empress Hotel.

Nowhere is the English atmosphere that permeates Victoria felt more keenly than in the Empress lobby each afternoon from 3:00 to 5:00 p.m. The ceremony of high tea dates back to the hotel's opening in 1908. You sense the importance of tea and crumpets when a sign "Closed for tea" at the grand entrance forces guests to use the East Porte Cochere.

Named after Britain's young queen in 1843, Victoria retains an old world charm. Baskets of flowers hang from cluster-lighted lamp posts. A quaint horse-drawn tally-ho and a doubledecker bus are delightful ways to view Canada's city of gardens. Roses bloom everywhere. Nasturtiums, pansies, poppies, even flowers you can't name grow in glorious profusion.

By sunlight or evening illumination, you can stroll through famous Butchart Gardens. Acres of flowers, shrubbery, rockeries, fountains and pools are the delight of nature lovers. Musical and dramatic entertainment enhance the flora and fauna on summer evenings.

A real "must" is the scenic Marine Drive winding closely around Oak Bay. Gorgeously landscaped homes are cantilevered on the rocks. Each curve unveils a spectacular natural seascape. Oak Bay Beach Hotel with Tudor architecture, colorful gardens and unexcelled views is a great place to stay if you don't mind being 15 minutes out of town.

Sealand, Canada's largest oceanarium is three fathoms beneath the sea. But more alluring to me than its killer whales and performing seals is nearby Oak Bay Marine Restaurant. Dinner in this glass enclosed restaurant is a sparkling interlude. Delightful decor in shades of blue melds into broad expanses of sea and sky with dancing gulls and scurrying sails—the food is good, too!

Downtown Victoria is a shopping mecca for connoisseurs of bone china, crystal, fine woolens and antiques. Attractive shops along the streets and tucked in arcades offer quality items at reasonable prices.

Historic buildings framing Bastion Square have been restored into a singularly pleasant shopping and dining complex. Its raised terrace overlooking the harbor is a lovely setting for lunchtime concerts. For a super lunch in a special place, try Chauney's. Just wait until you've tasted their poached salmon with hollandaise sauce—you'll probably go back for dinner as I did.

Meticulous attention to detail is evident in "Miniature World." A panorama of "tiny" people from fairy tales and history appeals to all ages. Other attractions include a wax museum and an underwater garden. But the true enchantment of Victoria is its jewel-like setting, old gabled houses, castles, massive flowers and fabulous views of the sea.

If you like to stay in a place reeking with atmosphere, take a look at Old England Inn. Rooms are furnished with antiques, some have canopied Royal beds. But whether you sleep here or not, be sure to sample a leisurely English breakfast, lunch or tea. Adjoining the Inn is a replica of Shakespeare's birthplace and Anne Hathaway's thatched cottage.

Rent a car and go exploring. I would suggest taking a lunch. Restaurants are few and far between while picnic areas and camping grounds are plentiful.

The scenery is spectacular north of Victoria. Mountains are spiked with towering 1,000 year old Douglas firs. An occasional primitive Indian village, or maybe a logging camp, and a few scattered fishing villages are tucked in the forested hillsides. From a few well-spaced lookouts, you can see hauntingly beautiful winding fjords. Log carriers and ferries look like toy boats in the emerald waters.

The hour and a half ferry ride from Victoria to Vancouver is breathtaking. Gliding through placid waterways, you pass fishing boats and catch a glimpse of life on some of the densely wooded islands which dip straight into the sea. Suddenly you spy the glittering skyline of Vancouver, dwarfed by snow-crusted mountain peaks.

# # #

Picture a spectacular setting: curtains of spiraling snow-iced mountains, footlights of silvery beaches encircling sparkling blue waters and props like ships, sylvan parks and glistening skyscrapers. No place quite like it—that's Vancouver.

An aerial tram ride to Grouse Mountain (3,700 ft.) is a splendid way to get the full impact of this awesome panorama. You can either ski down or return the same way after dining in the clouds.

To feel the city's flavor and view it close up, you must take a bus ride through Stanley Park. No ordinary park this—it's the only park I know with a view of the sea in every direction. Jutting into Buccard Inlet, this 1,000 acre wooded peninsula is a small world unto itself! The park has an aquarium, a zoo, beaches, swimming pools, restaurants, picnic grounds, a miniature railway, playing fields and 27 miles of trails for hiking and biking. You'll get a kick out of watching "properly" attired ladies and gentlemen bowling on the green.

It's also fun to meander through Gas Town. At one time considered the wrong side of the tracks, it is now being restored into a chic and "arty" section with boutiques, galleries, antiques and restaurants. At the "Meatyard," you are invited to grill your own steak. Soup and cheesecake are specialties in many of the sidewalk cafes. Some folks brown-bag it from one of the delis and saunter merrily on their way.

Canada's largest Chinese community (second largest in North America) is located near Gas Town. Enough curio shops, markets and restaurants to please the most discriminating Oriental connoisseurs.

Granville Mall is a walking plaza in the center of town. Cut off from most traffic, this leisurely tree-lined mall invokes the personal charm of European cities. Robsonstrasse, in the heart of downtown, comprises a four-block area of European shops. Interested in something German, Hungarian, Austrian, Danish or Greek? Include Robson Street on your itinerary.

Vancouver has its share of museums and cultural activities. In summer there are theatrical productions under the stars. Again, I find the ultimate appeal of this fascinating city in its sensational setting which few other cities in the world can equal. Facing water and backed by glaciers, it compels even the most sophisticated traveler to "ooh" and "ahh."

The North West Shore is a residential area across Lion's Gate Bridge. Gorgeous homes and gardens are contoured around the side of a mountain. From the highest road you can look back over all of Vancouver and its story-book setting. Lion's Gate Bridge is also the entranceway to Highway 99 which takes you through some wild terrain, fringed by mountains, to glacier-fed Garibaldi Lake and Garibaldi Provincial Park.

A great hotel is situated a few minutes from Stanley Park, right on one of the most stunning harbors in the world. Bayshore Inn has its own lush gardens and Trader Vic's Restaurant. You can charter a boat or plane at the adjacent marina.

But if you really want to be "transported," take their free chauffeur-driven Cadillac to the Vancouver Railroad Station. Board the 5:30 pm. Canadian Pacific Railroad and head for Banff. You'll arrive at 1:00 pm the next day and thank me for urging you to take this trip on what I call "Shangrila Express."

126

BANFF AND LAKE LOUISE
TAKE THE SHANGRI-LA EXPRESS

"ALL ABOARD!" THE CONDUCTOR'S signal echoed nostalgic memories. I hadn't rushed down a track scanning train car numbers since, oh well, a long, long time. But here I was at the Vancouver Railroad Station and there it was—car 291.

A porter arranged my luggage in the compartment and pointed to the dining car and observation roof. These glass domed cars which afford such visional freedom are the only place I know where travelers don't mind being tourists. And no wonder!

Breathtaking, a word often used carelessly, should be reserved for a really phenomenal visual experience. The train trip from Vancouver to Banff is just that! The Canadian Pacific Railroad, literally carved through miles of unparalleled beauty, is one continuous spectacle of splendor.

Don't bother packing playing cards or scrabble to while away the time; just take along some Murine for your eyes. I'm not kidding, my eyes actually ached from so much scenic grandeur. Even so, I resented each time my eyelids blinked.

Although food is good on the train and you can window-gaze from the dining car, it's a good idea to take your own picnic lunch. Get ensconced in the front seat of the observation car immediately. Settle back with a little cheese, some fruit and a bottle of wine, then start feasting your eyes on nature's marvels.

The track threads its slow way through constantly changing landscapes. Crystal crowns of snow atop majestic mountain peaks, vast stands of towering evergreens pierced by cascading waterfalls, snow-patched alpine meadows surprisingly ablaze with wildflowers, emerald green lakes pocketed in jagged rock, glacier-gorged valleys—and with each mile of railroad track, another spectacular view!

Fourteen years it took to build this unbelievable steel passage. Each of its 2500 miles is riveted in turbulent, romantic history. Read the triumphant saga of adventurous exploration and construction in Pierre Berton's "The Impossible Railway."

Fortunately, the sun doesn't set in the Canadian Rockies until after 10 pm and rises again about 4 am. By the time the slow-fading light embraces the silvered majesty of peak-studded wilderness, you are ready for bed.

Beauty doesn't fade during the few hours of darkness. As dawn filtered through the window, my first sight was a sparkling tiara of snow atop lofty-peaked alps. I dressed feverishly and raced back up to my vantage point. There's a camaraderie in observation cars rarely sensed among strangers. The thrill has to be shared. Those who have made the trip before are eager to let you know. One lady was reliving the scenic wonder through the eyes of her grandchildren. Even the conductor generated enthusiasm. "Oh, you can't leave now," he exclaimed as I was about to descend for breakfast. "In a minute you can look back and see both the tunnel entrance and exit in the mountain we just circled." Sure enough, there on different levels of the formidable solid rock were two dark, gaping cavities. The scope of this engineering feat staggers the imagination.

Banff was my destination, but when I learned the train stopped at Lake Louise, I decided to get off. Lake Louise is a jewel. I can understand why Indian

128

superstition used to forbid going near the lake. They were afraid the awesome beauty would strangle. The Canadian Pacific defied this folklore when they built Chateau Lake Louise. A legendary castle, the hotel, set amid cathedral spires of snow, is mirrored in the jade-green lake. Framed by glorious snow peaks, its grounds are a garden of golden poppies and nasturtiums.

Icefield Highway leads north to Jasper and south to Banff. Glacial patterns are silhouetted against a vast sky for 140 dramatic miles. Some resemble fortress cities. Others appear as giant cathedrals. Turquoise lakes are cradled between massive granite mountains. White rushing waterfalls, trickling streams and winding glacier-green rivers may be a photographer's paradise. But pictures can't capture the enchantment.

Enough magnificent superlatives. You must know I'm overwhelmed with the splendor of the Canadian Rockies. I can barely imagine the added thrill of being a skier in this snowy Eden. Here you can enjoy the longest ski season in North America.

Snowtime and summertime are equally fascinating at Banff. For those not content to gaze and rave, there is a galaxy of activity. Hikes with park guides and horseback trips along scenic trails are increasingly popular. Fishing, golf, swimming and tennis are great. A variety of programs and study courses in arts and crafts are offered at the Banff Centre School of Fine Arts. A two-week Festival of the Arts during August includes opera, ballet and drama.

Aerial trams whisk you up where you can dine amid glittering glaciers. It is possible to bathe in hot sulfur springs and shop at an Indian Trading Post. Outside of Jasper there's even a river raft tour which follows the old fur traders' canoe route.

Many modern motels with luxurious accommodations line Main Street. Bow View Inn is off the main drag, but has nice rooms with balconies overlooking Bow River. Banff Springs Hotel is a distinguished landmark, where you must go at least for a meal and to look at its medieval architecture. Stone floors, carved furniture and decorations of 16th century armor enhance its old-world charm.

Believe me, the fabulous trip from Vancouver to Banff is a "Shangrila Express."

Beltway Getaways around the Nations Capital

VII

WASHINGTON–SOME NOT-SO-USUAL ATTRACTIONS

Washington IS THE PULSE of the nation—a big, sprawling, resplendent city with something for everyone. Historical monuments, architectural triumphs and suburban serenity meld into a vibrant, metropolitan area connected by bridges and beltways.

Reams have been written about this fabulous city. Tourist guides swarm around the White House and Capitol. Everyone can find the Supreme Court and Lincoln Memorial. But a couple of new stellar attractions have been added to the tourist circuit, a few goodies are sort of tucked away from the main arteries and, geographically, Washington is located ideally for taking some cozy getaways.

A great way to start exploring the city is to visit the National Heritage Theater on 13th Street, one-half block from Pennsylvania Avenue. The American Adventure is brand new. In fact, it is a totally new "state of the art" combining motion pictures, super slides and special effects plus music composed especially for the show by Wayne Dirksen of the Washington National Cathedral. The exciting story of people and events that shaped a nation is narrated by William Conrad, star of the "Cannon" television series. The key to this dramatic 45 minute presentation is that the audience "experiences" the heritage, excitement, humor and grandeur of a nation as life-size images are projected onto 72 feet of curved screen. The American Adventure opened in January of 1976 and is presented in twin theaters from 8:30 am to 8:00 pm daily, March through October, and 11:00 am to 7:00 pm, November through February.

132

The Smithsonian, grand-daddy of museums, and the National Gallery of Art are well-known musts. But don't overlook the Corcoran Gallery of Art, highlighting American painters (17th and New York Avenue, N.W.), the Phillips Collection (1600 21st Street, N.W.), which emphasizes modern art, the Portrait Gallery (8th and F Streets, N.W.), a memorial to great Americans, and the newly-opened, unusually designed Hirshhorn Museum and Sculpture Garden (8th and Independence). The Renwick Gallery of the National Collection of Fine Arts, formerly the U.S. Court of Claims, is next to Blair House at 17th and Pennsylvania, N.W. The Renwick displays continuously changing exhibits of American crafts, design and architecture.

In addition to the magnificent John F. Kennedy Center with its Eisenhower Theater, Opera House, Concert Hall and American Film Institute, Washington's oldest and at one time only legitimate theater, The National, is still alive. Washington's own professional resident company stages outstanding productions at the Arena Stage and Kreeger Theater (6th and M Streets, S.W.) and Ford's Theatre, 501 10th Street, N.W., site of Lincoln's assassination has recently been restored.

Music is one of Washington's best bargains. Many concerts are free. Concerts are held in art galleries, libraries, churches and parks. The U.S. Army, Navy, Air Force and Marine Bands play on the steps of the East Front of the Capitol Building Monday, Tuesday, Wednesday and Friday nights at 8:00 pm. A calendar in the Style section of Friday's *Washington Post* and Sunday's *Washington Star* lists artists, times and dates.

Among the most colorful summertime events are the dramatic Marine Corps Parades. Performing under spectacular spotlights, the Marine Band, the Drum & Bugle Corps, the Silent Drill Platoon and the Marching Marines put on quite a show each Friday night at 8:00 pm from May 'til September. Marine

Barracks, 8th and I Streets, S.E. Call 543-1601 for free reserved seating. On Tuesday nights at 7:30 pm the Marine Corps presents a 45-minute parade on the grounds of the Iwo Jima Marine Corps Memorial in Arlington, Virginia.

Few people realize that some of the Foreign Policy Briefings held at the State Department are open to the public. Scheduled at 9:30 am on Tuesdays and Fridays, these interesting lectures, including a time for questions, last about an hour. Access to the East entrance is at 21st Street and Virginia Avenue, N.W.

Georgetown is an "experience" unto itself. Reeking with atmosphere, crammed full of galleries, shops, restaurants and people—well, you'll just have to discover Georgetown for yourself.

For a quiet, romantic oasis right in the heart of Georgetown, visit the gardens at Dumbarton Oaks. Entrance by way of Lovers' Lane between 30th and 31st Streets. You'll revel in waterfalls, wild flowers and formal gardens in a sylvan setting.

Don't forget that Washington's National Cathedral is just a few blocks north of Georgetown. It is the 6th largest cathedral in the world and one of the most beautiful. Located on the highest point of land in the District, its inspiring lines can be seen from miles away.

The largest Catholic Church in the United States is the National Shrine of the Immaculate Conception located at 4th Street and Michigan Avenue, N.E.—a magnificent combination of contemporary design and Byzantine and Romanesque architecture. Stained windows, intricate mosaics and carved stone statues are among its treasures.

Reminiscent of Medieval days is the Franciscan Monastery (14th and Quincy, N.E.). Visitors of all faiths enjoy its chapels and grottoes which are replicas of Holy Land shrines. Beneath the Memorial Church a narrow passageway is patterned after the Roman catacombs. Protiumcula Chapel is copied from the one where St. Francis of Assisi established the Franciscan Order in 1209. Ivy-covered rose gardens surrounding the Monastery form a peaceful setting for private meditating.

Not far from these restful gardens, you can visit Washington's National Arboretum (28th and M Streets, N.E.). Azaleas and rhododendrons at their peak (mid-April through May) are among the highlights. But you will find the extensive grounds enjoyable year-round. Ferns and wild-flowers are as beautifully preserved as majestic trees and exotic flowers. For year-round enjoyment the arboretum contains one of the most outstanding collections of conifers in North America.

Washington offers a wide selection of restaurants. A new establishment opens almost every week. You can eat on rooftops, in sidewalk cafes, underground, on boats, in Oriental splendor, sophisticated elegance or casual Bohemian. For an unusual menu of health food specialties try The Golden Temple at 1521 Connecticut Avenue, N.W. (if you can eat without a smoke). If you are looking for a raw bar with flair, go to Jack's Back Alley Raw Bar in the basement of The Greenery (1144 18th Street, N.W.). For the best view in town, try Top of the Town across Key Bridge in Rosslyn's Prospect House (1200 North Nash). And for an out-of-the-way intimate but unusual restaurant that's been around a long time, try the Iron Gate Inn. (1734 N Street, N.W., 1/2 block East of Connecticut Avenue). Set behind 19th century townhouses, the main dining room was originally a carriage house. Antique fireplaces are a-crackle in snappy weather. On warmer days and evenings you can dine in a courtyard surrounded by Magnolia trees and rose bushes in the shadows of the Byzantine dome of St. Matthew's Cathedral.

Washington abounds in exclusive department stores, specialty shops and boutiques. Many cities have branches of Saks Fifth Avenue, Lord and Taylor and

Neiman-Marcus, but only Washington has Garfinkels (14th and G Streets, N.W.). This elegant store remains the favorite of many Washingtonians.

Les Champs also provides distinctive shopping. Thirty attractive boutiques in the Watergate complex merge into one fabulous shopping center. Names like Gucci, Valentino and Cardin have expensive tags, but for 25¢ you can buy a souvenir Watergate bug! Want something really different? Visit Boutique Africa in the Museum of African Art. This unique gift shop sells African fabrics, jewelry, musical instruments, rugs and sculpture.

There is literally no end to activities and attractions in Washington. Eloquently combining big city advantages with small town pleasures, Washington epitomizes the best of environment, education, entertainment and enjoyment.

ALEXANDRIA –CITY OF CHARISMA

"A SMALL TRADING PLACE IN ONE of the finest situations imaginable."
This brief description of Alexandria made in 1759 applies equally today. In the
shadows of Washington, D.C. Alexandria exudes the spirit of early America
while emitting a flavor of old Europe. Picturesque tree-canopied streets, some
paved with cobblestones, quaint shops and galleries, stunning architecture and
unique restaurants add to the charisma of this historic Potomac riverport.

Alexandria is a "free" city—one of the three in America that is not a part
of a county. More than that, most of its historic homes and shrines are free to
the public. One of the favorite attractions which doesn't cost a cent is walking
through "Old Town" to view beautifully restored 18th and 19th Century homes.
Here you will find more homes of this period, privately restored as residences,
than in any town in Virginia—more than in Philadelphia, for that matter.

Mellow is the atmosphere permeating Alexandria's Old Town. Colonial
style courtyards lend an appealing aura. Sometimes used for band concerts and
art fairs, Market Square with elevated terraces and fountains is a sequestered
oasis in the heart of town. Get some cheese and a bottle of wine on the corner
(at Hickory Farms) and have lunch on a shaded bench.

Ramsay House, open daily, is the city's oldest house. A delightful garden
adjoins the yellow clapboard house built in 1724. A color film clues you in on
not-to-be-missed buildings and parks and sets the stage for your sojourn in
George Washington's hometown. Guided walking tours originate here with maps,

137

brochures and free parking passes.

Captain's Row is a must (the 100 block of Prince Street.) It exemplifies Alexandria's Scottish origin. Quaint houses, built by seafaring captains, line a cobblestone road to the waterfront.

The Old Presbyterian Meeting House, built in 1774 by the Scottish founders, has had an active congregation since its church bell began tolling at the news of George Washington's death. Washington's funeral services were conducted in the chapel of the Meeting House although he worshipped at Christ Church at Cameron and North Washington Street. Here you can see the pews owned by both George Washington and Robert E. Lee. And within a stone's throw of the Washington Monument tombs of confederate soldiers fill the bricked-in churchyard. You can enjoy an organ recital each Wednesday at noon in the small chapel.

Imposing George Washington National Masonic Memorial on King Street contains vast memorabilia of Colonial treasures. Included is an ivory-handled trowel used by President Washington to lay the cornerstone of the Capitol in 1793. Actually, this site with an unsurpassed view over Washington was originally proposed for the National Capitol Building. Stained glass windows and dioramas depict events in Washington's life.

The most complete collection of antique drugstore furnishings and handblown glass containers in the nation is to be found at Stabler-Leadbeter Apothecary Shop which looks just as it did when patronized by Martha Washington.

An excellent example of Georgian architecture is Gadsby's Tavern, 128 North Royal Street. The picturesque courtyard looks much as it did when it harbored stagecoaches. Once a center for Alexandria's social life, this 18th century tavern is being restored as a working tavern in the colonial tradition.

Alexandria is not just history. Utilizing an old torpedo factory used during World War I and II, the Bicentennial Committee has created a new art center. Day and evening art classes are offered year-round. Workshops, studios and galleries in this old waterfront building at King and Union Streets contain the work of modern painters, sculpturs, potters, jewelry makers, lithographers and silkscreen painters. You will have difficulty browsing without buying.

I must tell you something else. The Virginia Museum of Fine Arts has its headquarters in one of the city's two neoclassic Greek Revival buildings. I mention this as much for the outstanding organization as the imposing Athenaeum building.

The George Washington Bicentennial Center occupies the other important Greek Revival building at 201 North Washington Street. A dramatic audio-visual interpretation of Alexandria's role in the American Revolution is presented continuously. Handmade 18th Century reproductions and colonial prints and drawings are for sale.

On St. Asaph Street is the Old Town Common. A variety of shops includes the Greek Boutique. Hand-crocheted clothing, handsome gold-filled jewelry and fur bedspreads highlight the collection. Randy Parris designs her own creations.

Alexandria shopping is an around-the-globe adventure. Iberian Imports features artistic furnishings from Spain and Portugal. Dockside and Pier I boast an inventory from around the world, while the Glockenspiel, Irish Walk, Tartan and Scandinavian Too are self-explanatory.

Over a hundred unique shops and galleries in charming old houses strive for and achieve individuality. To prove it there's a Gallery of Animal Art (803 King Street) with etchings, porcelains, sculpture, lucite and woodcarvings—artisans will duplicate your favorite animal in every conceivable media.

Antiques and Alexandria are almost synonomous. But Wilfred Rogers on

King Street caters to the modern taste with an emphasis on elegance.

Several old Alexandria warehouses have been converted into attractive restaurants. King's Landing serves French cuisine in a colonial setting. The Wharf broils excellent rock fish and generally specializes in fresh seafood. The Warehouse features "historic" hamburgers and sandwiches. L'Estaminet is a new café on North Washington Street. A delicious selection of quiches go particularly well with a cold bottle of French beer. Ice cream cones go everywhere. People stroll along the streets and through the plazas with their cones. The Old Town Confectionary with it's ice cream parlor has them lined up every day at 210 King Street. My favorite is dispensed from a small window behind Il Porto Restaurante at the corner of Lee and King Street. Try their pistachio—it's great!

History buffs, antique collectors, and others will enjoy reconoitering the streets of Old Town Alexandria.

SUNWORSHIPERS ARE OFTEN in too big a hurry as they head for the popular beaches on Maryland's Eastern Shore. Slow down! You are missing some of the most historic and picturesque villages in the state. Why, just a five-mile by-pass off Route 50, 33 miles from the Bay Bridge, takes you through tiny, quaint Wye Mills. From a car window you can see America's largest and oldest white oak tree. Known as the Wye Oak, Maryland's official state tree stands 95 feet tall with a spread of 165 feet and a 21-foot circumference. Extensive open-trunk surgery is evident on this magnificent 450-year-old specimen. Its gnarled limbs are more the size of average trees. Another tree in the old churchyard is no sapling. Oaks really grow big around here.

Wye Church dates back to the early 1700's. Among its interesting features are high box pews, a hanging pulpit, the west gallery, which bears the Royal Arms of England, and a 1937 silver communion service. You can also see an 18th century grist mill still in operation. The mill's chief claim to fame is grinding flour for Washington's troops at Valley Forge. A 19th century one-room red schoolhouse completes the tour of Wye Mills and a curve later you are back on Route 50.

Take an hour's detour and drive through lovely, old Easton. Referred to as "the Colonial Capital of the Eastern Shore," Easton is the county seat of Talbot. New construction adheres to a Colonial-style architecture, so Easton retains a charming period atmosphere.

For a meal or a vacation, you will reval in the stately Tidewater Inn. Although a completely modern hotel, the "red-coat service" and traditional Maryland food are geared to the hospitality associated with Publick Houses of Colonial times. Whether your idea of relaxing is a swim, a set of tennis, unique shops or a thirst-quencher in an English flavored tavern—you'll find diversion at Tidewater Inn.

If you have a little more time, turn right at Route 333 and drive into Oxford. Originally a bustling seaport for international shipping, Oxford is now a busy yachting center, especially popular with sailboat enthusiasts. You can browse around colorful shipyards or stroll through quiet, tree-canopied streets.

The Robert Morris Inn, long associated with Oxford, recaptures the architectural heritage of early America. In a beautiful dining room with dramatic murals and crystal chandeliers, sumptuous meals are served in the gracious tradition of long ago. An adjoining tavern with warm wood-pegged walls, brick fireplaces and a slate floor is a charming place to try a different beverage—say, for instance, a blackberry or apricot sour. I had already ordered a draft beer before I learned about these unusual specialties. A red-coated waiter happily gave me the recipe to try at home. In case you are curious, use your favorite fruit flavored brandy blended with a sour mix and serve on crushed ice! Upstairs bedrooms in this 18th century residence are furnished with antiques. Some of the four-poster beds have to be reached by steps.

Right outside this historic inn is the oldest free running ferry in the United States. You can cross Tred Avon River in a couple of minutes and make an immediate return or take your car (it holds three) and leisurely proceed to St. Michael's, a small fishing village nestled around a secluded harbor. Its sheltered waters lure sportsmen year-round. St. Michaels is really a working as well as a pleasure harbor. It is used by oystermen, crabbers, clammers and fishermen.

142

Waterfront restaurants feature its freshly caught seafood and cater to diners by land or by sea. Coq Au Vin on Main Street is a delightful French restaurant enriching the culinary scene.

St. Michaels' harbor is the site of the Chesapeake Maritime Museum, complete with a lighthouse, a light ship, a skip-jack and other old fishing vessels. A boardwalk-type train originates here for a tour of the 300-year old town.

A sightseeing boat cruises along peaceful Miles River. Many old mansions and modern homes afford a glimpse into the gracious way of life which has been retained in this scenic slow-paced area.

Attractive shops offer appealing items for all tastes. At the Gingerbread House you can find handmade dresses from handwoven fabrics. Handcarved birds and waterfowl are the specialty at The Duck's Nest. Ed Burns carves and his wife paints with artistic realism in their home on Bosman Road, Route 579.

Something new looms on St. Michael's skyline—Martingham Harbour-towne Inn. Although large in scope and modern in design, this unique vacation-conference center preserves the beauty and simplicity which typifies Tidewater country elegance. It fits right into the scheme of things while providing luxurious accommodations and beautiful dining rooms with spectacular waterfront views. Whether staying in a single room or a large lodge with kitchen and living room, you can enjoy golf, tennis, swimming, biking, hiking, hunting and fishing—it's all here at Harbourtowne Inn.

On your way to the beach stopover on Maryland's Eastern Shore. Explore some of the quaint villages, picturesque harbors and historic landmarks which are so near—just a few turns off the beach path.

Directions: I-95 to Exit 31-Route 50, across Bay Bridge.

Although there are no pumpkins in Morven Park, even Cinderella would be delighted with the unique carriage museum. More than 75 horsedrawn vehicles, including coaches, sulkies, buggies, sleighs and Victorian carriages are appropriately displayed in the original carriage house of this spacious estate. These service vehicles of yesteryear are effectively exhibited with harnesses, lamps, miniature models, pictures and other livery.

Located two miles north of Leesburg, Morven Park encompasses 1,200 acres with a handsome Greek Revival style mansion, outstanding boxwood gardens and winding nature trails. During the Civil War, Confederate troops were stationed at this historic park. Today a trust fund established by former Governor and Mrs. Davis preserves the showplace for historical and cultural interests An International Esquestrian Institute is also located on its extensive grounds. A "coaching" day is held each fall at Morven Park and it is an exhilarating spectacle to see a single buggy or stately four-in-hand coach rolling over the beautiful lawns.

The tempo of this quiet Southern town, Leesburg, lends itself to a museum of this type. It is easy to visualize yesterday's carriage rides through the tree-lined streets of quaint fieldstone houses and federal-style buildings. Today you can view some of these structures dating back to 1757 by either a walking tour or a windshield tour.

144

Courthouse Square with its historic elm shaded lawn and the Loudoun Museum, a log cabin originally built in 1764 as a silversmith's shop, are two of the key attractions. Among the interesting items found in this miniature gallery, are a blue velvet dress worn by Mrs. Lincoln, Confederate Presidential ballots of 1861 and a collection of antique toys.

Designed to carry you back to old Virginny, The Green Tree is a rare restaurant serving elegant 18th century food and spirits. Few Colonial-style restaurants have appealed to me more. For a memorable dining experience, have dinner, lunch or brunch in one of the Green Tree's two charming dining rooms. Candles and firelight flicker over brick floors, cherry paneling and old pewter. Chamber music and costumed waitresses enhance the genial ambience. It takes a talented and dedicated chef to reproduce food exactly as it was in Virginia's great houses. The Green Tree has one with enthusiasm. They bake fresh Sally Lunn bread every morning, make their own unusual soups and desserts and stick meticulously to ingredients and recipes used 200 years ago. Appropriate vintage wines and fanciful after-dinner drinks are part of the easy, leisurely charm. Dedicated to authentic 18th century cuisine and atmosphere, The Green Tree is a delightful addition to Leesburg (15 South King Street, 703/777-7246).

Located next door to the Green Tree, the Leesburg Clothes Horse emphasizes classic clothes and quality accessories. In the rear you'll find the Country Store, full of unusual imports and local items, a fun store.

Another shopping adventure reminiscent of days gone by awaits you nearby at The Country Butcher, a market completely devoid of cellophane packages. Meats are displayed in an old-fashioned meat case. Don't dare go home without a country ham and some of their freshly made sausage.

For a beautiful drive and unexpected surprise, continue out of Leesburg on Route 7 and make a sharp right turn immediately after crossing the bridge over the Shenandoah River. Follow a winding, wooded country road along the river for two miles and discover the secluded Holy Cross Monastery. This 1,200 acre estate, once a Civil War Battleground, is now the peaceful home of 33 Trappist Monks. Here they are engaged in a self-study program directed by an Episcopal Minister from Washington. A Jewish psychiatrist conducts workshops on analysis and sensitivity training.

The monks of Our Lady of the Holy Cross combine spirituality with industry as they breed Black Angus cattle and operate a bakery which produces the popular small loaves of "Monastery Bread." Bells of the Monastery chapel call the monks to prayer eight times daily. Peace and tranquility pervade this small, pristine church as Gregorian chants reverberate throughout the hall. Its doors are open to the public at all times.

After this refreshing retreat, it is befitting to wend your way home by way of Waterford, a restored Quaker village dating back to 1733. This charming town is the scene of the famed three-day annual Home Tour and crafts exhibit held the first weekend in October, but a stroll through the quiet streets is enjoyable any time of the year. The Corner Store and The Mill, two landmarks of Waterford, are open on the weekends from June through October.

Follow Route 655 a couple of miles to Whites Ferry, famed for General Robert E. Lee's crossing with his troops during the Civil War. It is the last ferry boat in operation on the Potomac. Returning home by this ancient mode of transportation adds the final touch of tranquility to this tranquil beltway getaway.

Directions: Take Exit 10 and follow Route 7. Morven Park is open April through October, 10am to 5pm, Sundays 1pm to 5pm. Closed Mondays and Tuesdays. Adults $1.75, children 75¢

Westminister, IN THE HEART OF MARYLAND'S lush farmland, maintains a living monument to the sturdy people who contributed greatly to today's agricultural economy. Frankly, the idea of a Farm Museum didn't really excite me, but I decided to take a look. What a pleasant surprise! The Carroll County Farm Museum is no ordinary museum. It captures and translates early farm life, a way of life that was simple but good—when farms were self-sustaining, when farmers raised their own crops, canned and preserved, made their own tools, raised cattle and hogs for their meat and made the family clothing of spun wool from their sheep.

Costumed guides show visitors through the main farm house which is an excellent example of Civil War period construction. Five rooms are furnished as they were in the late 1800's. Of particular interest is the kitchen with huge fireplace and cooking pots. Every type of early farm equipment is displayed throughout the 140-acre complex. Wander through barns, animal pens, a smokehouse, springhouse and blacksmith shop (still operating on Saturdays and Sundays). Craft demonstrations on weekends include spinning, weaving, broom-making and churning.

Nature trails, a garden and shaded tables near a lake provide a delightful spot for a picnic. If you didn't pack a lunch (and providing it's Saturday), you're still in luck. Adjacent to the farm museum is a farmer's market where you can select fresh produce and bakery products, even hot dogs, pizza and sandwiches.

You may be so inspired with nostalgia of the "good old days" that you'll want to buy enough fruits and vegetables to do some "jarring." A schedule of demonstrations is a part of the farmer's market program. Depending on the date, you may watch cake decorating, canning, quilting, needlework or leathercraft. They will also teach you how to make ice cream, yeast bread, barbecued meats and sand terrariums. For additional information on the market, call 301/346-7789.

For the more sophisticated diner, Route 140 into Reistertown is teeming with country inns. Everyone in Westminister has high praise for "The Country Fair," especially if you like quiche lorraine. I did enjoy their quiche, as well as the ambience of the old structure which dates back to 1750. Nearby Forest Inn also radiates a warm atmosphere. The bartender assured us this was the best place of all to eat and seemed disappointed when we left after one of his well-mixed drinks. But I wanted to visit one of the two restaurants back in Westminster. Angelo's and Cocky's Tavern are open only in the evening and are excellent. The Tavern is an attractively restored townhouse.

For fun shopping or browsing, stop at The Loafing Barn. The interior of a restored barn on the edge of town is filled with an interesting assortment of antiques, art, imports, jewelry and specially designed clothing. This unusual shop is open from May through December (weather permitting) from Noon to 5pm, except Monday and Friday.

On the opposite end of town, Western Maryland College, referred to as "The Hill," was founded in 1867 as the first coed liberal arts college south of the Mason-Dixon Line. Rolling hills on its 160-acre campus contain a 9-hole golf course which is open to visitors as well as students.

Unlike most small towns reflecting simplicity of earlier days, West-minister's courthouse is not the traditional city center. In fact, I had a hard time finding the charming old Court House Square. Located one block off Main Street on Court Street, the handsome classic revival building with a two-story portico and hexagonal cupola is shaded by immense pines and elms.

It was in Westminister where America's first countrywide system of Rural Free Delivery was established. You will find an unusual exhibit of early pioneer mailcarrying at Historic House (206 East Main Street). It contains, in addition to the Postal Museum, some 150 antique dolls, a unique collection of American flags and an assortment of tools and implements used before the Machine Age. Built in 1807, this original old home is appropriate headquarters for the County Historical Society.

Union Mills, a few miles North on Route 140, is one of Maryland's oldest, most picturesque homes, preserving rural American life from days before the Civil War. Built in 1797 by Mr. Shriver who drew up the Rural Free Delivery plans adopted by the Post Office Department, the Homestead (still lived in) has served as a post office, store, courthouse, stagecoach station, school and Inn. Today the rambling 23-room house and adjoining mill comprise a living museum.

Whether your interests are geared to 19th century rural life, Civil War relics, architecture, antiques or country roaming, you'll enjoy visiting Carroll County, a step into yesterday.

Directions: I-95 to Exit 21, Route 97 and 32.

"OH, YOU *HAVE* TO GET LOST to find New Windsor," Robert Cairns assured me. I had just explained how lost I was on Maryland's country roads. But there are several roads and a couple of good reasons to go to New Windsor.

Quiet frankly, I stopped at the Boxwood Antique Shop for directions to The International Gift Shop. This proved a delightful detour. A sign, "Open—Please ring and wait a moment," intrigued me to do just that. Mr. Cairns graciously and leisurely showed me around. His garden is really more important to him than the store, at least he enjoys it more. With great pride he told me a little history of the rambling dwelling encircling the garden.

A one-room tavern built around 1790 grew into an eight-room log house. Additions were made in 1830 including bricking in a courtyard. By 1864 the Dielman Inn was a landmark at the junction of Buffalo and Monacacy Roads. Serving also as a cultural center, a wing of the Inn was used as a private school.

Having attended Miss Angie's "select" school from kindergarten to high school, Mrs. Cairns had a great affection for the Inn. In 1959 she and her husband acquired the building, remodeling one wing into an apartment and operating an antique shop on the ground level.

Spacious rooms contain an assortment of Carroll County antiques and a fascinating collection of handwoven coverlets. For more up-to-date items, there is an adjoining home and garden shop. The Inn's charming boxwood garden with a graceful, ivy-covered arbor designed in 1870 for the pleasure of summer guests, remains a refreshing oasis for visitors today.

It is hard to believe New Windsor was once a bustling resort town. Folks came from far and near to bathe in its famed hot sulfur springs. It's also hard to visualize 40,000 troops passing through its quiet streets on their way to Gettysburg in 1863. Like all small towns, New Windsor is proud of its historic heritage.

It has achieved religious recognition as the birthplace of Methodism. A tablet on the front door of an old cabin vouches that "Here Mr. Strawbridge formed the first Methodist Society in Maryland and America." A crude pulpit used in this tiny house for 41 years is thought to be the oldest Methodist pulpit. Currently it is in the Lane Museum in Baltimore.

Religious influence in New Windsor is not confined to history. I discovered that the International Gift Shop I was looking for is a part of the "Brethren Service Center." For exciting articles from around the world, you can shop in a spacious new building, save money and help combat poverty overseas at the same time.

The International Gift Shop is a nonprofit organization sponsored by SERRV (Sales Exchange for Refugee Rehabilitation Vocations). Developed as an outlet for overseas craftsmen, it is a self-help handicrafts marketing program. Hundreds of beautiful hand-crafted articles from over 30 nations are on display. They include decorated porcelains and brass from Hong Kong, ivory and mother of pearl jewelry from Jordan, teakwood carvings from Thailand, wooden bowls from Haiti, woolens from South America and exquisite hand-embroidered clothing. With their colorful mail order catalog, you can even shop from home. I was really impressed with both the quality workmanship and the discount prices.

I was also impressed with the friendly personnel and campus-like grounds, so I did some investigating and took a tour. The Brethren Service Center is owned and operated by the Church of the Brethren. Originally a college (from 1911 to 1937), the hilltop location on Main Street is now known as the New Windsor Service Center. It incorporates, besides the international gift shop, a clothing program, Interchurch Medical assistance, Lutheran world relief and the Church World Service. The Center serves as an attractive site for conferences, ecumenical world programs and retreats.

Four residence halls can accommodate up to a hundred people. Some air-conditioned rooms have private baths, others are dormitory style. Although individuals can use the Center's facilities for self-meditation retreats, it is primarily for groups averaging in number from 25 to 35. First come—first served, is the rule of order. Saturdays are devoted to day-conferences and a number of auditoriums can handle several hundred persons. Food is available. In fact, even if you are just there to shop, ask a saleslady to call for you. If there's enough food and the time is between 12:00 and 12:30, you can enjoy one of the best home-cooked meals imaginable. Hope you are lucky enough to go on a day when they have fresh vegetable soup. By the way, the Center is closed on Sundays.

All age groups are encouraged to participate in the Center's unusual programs which "represent the church working at practical expressions of a Christ-like spirit of brotherhood and reconciliation worldwide."

If your time budget or inclination isn't geared to an extended retreat, I feel sure you will find a day in the serene atmosphere of New Windsor to be a refreshing mini-retreat. So, get lost and go do New Windsor.

Directions: I-95 to Exit 18 to 270. Take Route 27 North to Route 407. Right on Route 31.

POTOMAC IS STRUGGLING TO RETAIN its artistic, serene and rural flavor in the midst of a surging population boom. Once a charming hamlet of working farms with a few horse lovers, a sprinkling of artists and a couple of shops, Potomac is now a vibrant community of beautiful homes, magnificent estates, large farms, interesting shops and stimulating people from all walks of life.

Miles of white board fences are the hallmark of Maryland's hunt country, paralleled by biking, hiking and riding trails. Located only 12 miles from Washington, Potomac beautifully combines leisurely country living with the diversity and vitality of the city.

Where else could you find a service station ministering to social as well as automotive needs? Well, just try to stop for gas any day at Mitch and Bill's without running into three of your best friends (that is, if you live in the area). Mitch and Bill's is the cornerstone of Potomac. Their Exxon station, which opened in 1949, was Potomac's first commercial establishment. Still operating at the same focal corner, which now boasts the only stop light in Potomac, Mitch and Bill have watched this unique area spring from a quiet country crossroad to a thriving, flourishing village.

Three banks and three beauty shops cater to financial and beauty needs of Potomacites, whose standard attire seems to be riding breeches, white tennis togs or pants. A couple of super shops can supply needs for dressier occasions, however. Perlhoff has a splendiferous selection of sophisticated casuals and for that something really different, try "On-the-Left-Bank."

Although a couple of the large chains have made their inroad (tastefully in keeping with the colonial atmosphere), it is still possible to shop in a friendly, privately owned grocery or drug store. You just can't duplicate the appeal of a small, neighborhood grocery where meat is fresh, not frozen and some of the old customers still keep a running charge account. This is true of the Potomac Super Market next to Mitch and Bill's.

I particularly enjoy the flavor of an intimate, old-fashioned drugstore. Potomac Village Pharmacy dispenses a nifty soda, maintains a tiny post office and features top-of-the-line items. The Yaffes take great pride in their "personal" drug store. They laugh about attending weddings of customers for whom "Doc" has filled baby prescriptions.

The Surrey and Camalier & Buckley are two gift shops with attractive and unusual items. The Surrey is headquarters for riding paraphernalia. Mixed with saddles and breeches you will find portraits by Migs Elliot. If you've never thought of having yours painted, you will after seeing her outstanding work.

You'll love the tantalizing aroma at The Danish Baker. If you sample a goodie at an old-timey ice cream parlor table or take yours home, be sure to try their fresh raspberry strudel.

Don't let the shack-like appearance dissuade you. In a 200-year-old building across from Mitch and Bill's, you'll find "Interiors by Edythe." Even Washington ambassadors have discovered Edythe. She sells rare antiques and curios and loans swatches of fabulous fabrics. Whether you have a mansion refurbished or a pillow recovered, you will benefit from her friendly decorating service.

Your landscaping needs may run to exotic shrubbery and trees or a single hanging basket, you'll find a complete inventory at the Potomac Garden Center on River Road.

A couple of restaurants with charm and romance have been popular since the Thirties. Old Angler's Inn at MacArthur Boulevard is an ancient stone house with a dimly lit panelled room where you can sip cocktails before an open fire. Up a shiplike wrought iron spiral staircase, you climb to the dining room. In summer, drinks and meals are served on a shaded patio.

Normandy Farms, out Falls Road, is a rambling, rustic country restaurant with a French flavor. Hot popovers and French onion soup have helped put this popular eatery on the map. Five fireplaces and an extensive array of old copper utensils create a mellow, easy-going atmosphere. There's music in the evenings.

The Chesapeake & Ohio Canal with its unique locks (Swain's and Pennifield, among others) and the roaring Great Falls, just minutes from Potomac, are great places for picnicking, boating, fishing and camping. This historic waterway once carried supplies of peace and war from the farmlands and foundries of Ohio to the nation's capital. There are towpaths for hiking and biking any season and when the canal is frozen, an open fire on the towpath and ice skating is a natural. A museum devoted to the history of the C&O Canal is located at Great Falls.

Cabin John Regional Park is nearby at Tuckerman Lane. Here 500 acres are geared to family recreation in a sylvan setting. Indoor tennis courts are around the corner on Democracy Boulevard and an 18-hole golf course on Falls Road are open to the public.

Potomac is and has been a Utopia for sports enthusiasts. Point-to-Point races attract spectators in droves and polo matches at Travilah are a sell-out in the summer. Hunting? Well, there's been everything from coon hunting in the early days to fashionable fox hunting today.

Carrying water from a spring may conjure a picture of long ago. But out near River Road (formerly an old Canayan Indian Trail) and Seven Locks Road, you'll see more and more jugs of fresh spring water being carried away by health conscious Potomacites.

Sure, Potomac is growing, but everyone who has moved there did so because they liked the way it was. That's really the way it still is—with the proper frame of mind.

Directions: I-95 to Exit 16.

Harpers Ferry, THE QUAINT and quiet town visited in the summer and fall for its gorgeous scenery and historic sightseeing, captures for one weekend in December the nostalgia of yesterday's Yuletide.

Steeped in American history and now in the process of being restored by the National Park Service, Harpers Ferry really retains the flavor of a bygone era. Its picturesque old stone, frame and brick buildings provide a perfect setting for a leisurely, truly old-time Christmas celebration.

Religious and folk groups perform at historic St. Patrick's Catholic Church. Throughout the evenings carollers stroll through the lamplit streets blending their voices with the merriment. Glowing fires in old wooden barrels add light as well as warmth along the route. "Put Christ back into Christmas" and "Happiness is an old-fashioned Christmas" are the joint themes of Harpers Ferry's Christmas jubilee. Abraham Lincoln and his family arrive by train and are met by the Mayor of Harpers Ferry. Costumed soldiers escort them to the National Armor's House where a string quartet plays 18th century music.

This captivating weekend might well be called a candlelight panorama. Every window throughout the village is bathed in candlelight and each shop is lighted by candles or kerosene lanterns. Even the famous old stone steps of St. Patrick's Church are the scene of a unique candle lighting ceremony.

Originality and authenticity are the keynotes for Christmas decorations and refreshments as shops and galleries compete for individuality. Salesladies

157

dress in authentic costumes dating back to 1860.

Daniel's General Store, with its extraordinary collection of calico and ginghams, features a tree full of calico baubles. Here the whole family gets into the act. Mrs. Daniel exhibits a vast assortment of beautiful quilts and her husband demonstrates colonial tinsmithing in his 200-year old tinsmith shop. Making authentic clothing worn during the Revolutionary and Civil War periods is the fascinating job of the Daniels' daughter. A variety of Pat's unique items, including bonnets and Jeb Stewart hats, are for sale.

Here, too, there are continuous demonstrations of exciting crafts. You can watch dazzling pieces of jewelry being created right before your eyes as George Flory demonstrates the wizardry of enameling on silver or copper. Or enjoy the pageantry of pottery unfold as Renni Parziole explains the development of his ancient craft.

Adjoining Daniel's General Store is a very appropriate shop for Christmas browsing—Starlight Dolls. Harriett Cavallero has put her love of dolls to great use by making and repairing all sorts of dolls. She specializes in reproducing antique dolls and painting porcelain. One dream doll with its cuddly body and porcelain face and arms and legs even has a real lace (dipped in porcelain) bonnet with tiny porcelain rose buds. Mrs. Cavallero also makes stuffed animals, as well as other unusual toys. A large doll house furnished to scale is on display and some of the miniature furniture is for sale. While you are deciding how many dolls to include on your Christmas list and revelling in the spectacular fresh cedar tree trimmed with dolls, you can enjoy homemade cookies and herbed tea.

Don't overlook Canal House. In this shop of fine antiques William Payne serves hot cider from a large kettle hanging right in his fireplace. At Audrey Preister's Art Gallery three floors of an old house are filled with excellent works. Another stop should include Stowell's Art Gallery.

Do today's children know what a taffy pull is? Well they will after a visit to the festive tent outside the Iron Horse Inn. Shirley Dougherty puts on a taffy pull Saturday afternoon. What could be more nostalgic than watching children pull their own taffy? Well, maybe popcorn balls—they were always my favorite! Popcorn strings, red ribbon bows and candles decorate the tree at the Iron Horse Inn.

The Hilltop House with its exceptional view of three states has been providing accommodations and family-style meals for years. It even boasts having been a favorite retreat of President Woodrow Wilson and Mark Twain. Just a mile away, Cliffside Motel, "a modern motel on the battlefield," offers all the comforts of home and Mr. and Mrs. Newcommer guarantee a good meal at any time.

Thomas Jefferson once said the view from Jefferson Rock behind St. Patrick's Church was worth a voyage across the Atlantic. I believe he would agree that a day or a weekend spent in this gracious atmosphere emphasizing the spiritual and traditional aspects of Christmas would certainly be well worth the drive from Washington.

Happy holidays at Harpers Ferry to you and yours!

Directions: Take Beltway 495 to Exit 17, continue on 70S to Harpers Ferry Exit. First weekend in December.

IN THE MIDST OF TODAY'S HECTIC holiday festivities, there remain a few remnants of an old-fashioned Christmas. For a meal, a day, a week or more, you and your family can enjoy a memorable holiday visit into the past at several nearby Inns.

Boar's Head Inn

Boar's Head Inn in Charlottesville, Virginia, revives one of the season's oldest customs, "Bringing in the Boar's Head Ceremony." Trumpets sound as the boar's head, a medieval symbol of hospitality, appears on an elaborate platter. Eighteenth-century dishes follow in profusion to the accompaniment of the ancient (1521) Boar's Head Carol.

This distinguished inn recalls the hospitality and social life enjoyed by Virginians many Christmases ago. Start your day with an eye-opening plantation breakfast or champagne brunch. Search for the Yule Log. Join in the madrigals and wassailing before an open fire. Revel in the colorful bonfires and fireworks. Have yourself a merry little Christmas in the atmosphere of Merrie Old England!

Williamsburg

Williamsburg, Virginia's Colonial capital, celebrates the Advent season for two exciting weeks with the merriment of traditions that have been cherished through the centuries. Townspeople share in the warm-hearted spirit as they creatively decorate their homes with beautiful natural garlands and greenery. Nights are aglow with candles.

From the Tagging of the Tree, an unusual welcoming ceremony to the King and Queen Dinner, with the cutting of the Queen's cake on New Year's Day, you can participate in a variety of activities associated with holidays of a bygone era.

Have you tried greased pole-climbing lately? Or how about shot-putting? Market Square is a perfect setting for these and other colonial sports. "Beating of the Holiday Drums," a colorful program of music and drills by costumed fifers and drummers, is staged on the village green.

The Groaning Board, a lavish colonial banquet with entertainment in the manner of yesteryear, and candlelight concerts in the ballroom of the Governor's Palace with costumed musicians are just a few of the events which enrich your experience of Christmas in Williamsburg.

Tides Inn

Tides Inn in Irvington, Virginia, comfortably blends old traditions with modern customs. Lavish decorations reflect a happy transition from old to new. Christmas carolers cruise through surrounding creeks and coves on a floating houseboat. Children from the local churches come to sing during the Yule Log ceremony on the afternoon of Christmas Eve. Santa Claus makes a stop after dinner with a gift for every guest. And for your last-minute shopping there is a terrific gift shop full of imports, antiques, toys—you name it, it's there.

Although the atmosphere is leisurely and serene in this magnificent but informal resort, a diversified program is planned to keep you amused—eggnog parties, pirate bingo, shipboard horse racing, dancing, to name a few. Even though the air is brisk, a luncheon cruise on The Tides' yacht, High Tide, is one of the most popular events at what many call America's most unusual inn.

Annapolis

A blithe, cheery spirit pervading the air in Annapolis is contagious during the Christmas holidays. Lamp posts, street signs, indeed the whole town, is bedecked with swags and wreaths of native greenery studded with red bows.

Many of the historic homes are appropriately decorated in the 18th-century manner. Rooms aglow with candlelight, hostesses in costume and chamber music express the dignity and gentility of the period as well as the festivity of the holidays. A fire crackles in the cooking fireplace of the brick-floored kitchen. Homemade brandy snaps, sugar cookies and wassail are served with the price of admission.

The elegant simplicity of garlands, wreaths and kissing balls made of fresh boxwood, holly, magnolia leaves and feathery evergreens inspires one to eliminate tinsel and glitter from modern ornaments and return to decorations of Christmases yore.

Maryland Inn, in keeping with its 200-year heritage, schedules three days of holiday feasts and festivities at Christmas time plus an annual 18th-century New Year's feast. During their traditional merriment you can enjoy madrigal singers, a harp concert during Christmas dinner and music by the famed guitarist, Charlie Byrd. Colonial meals include roast goose, roast beef with Yorkshire pudding, corn pudding, plum pudding and tipsy square. Spirits are as important to yuletime celebrating as food. Enjoy champagne with your breakfast, mulled wine for lunch and maybe end the day with the Farmer's Bishop? (Served in the countryside during the annual visit of the Bishop—"add Brandy to the capacity of the Bishop!")

A candlelight tour of historic Annapolis is enchanting on Christmas Eve. So is Christmas at the Market Place with its huge Christmas tree and dazzling glow from ships and boats in the harbor brightly lighted for the holidays. Other seasonal events in Annapolis include the "Messiah" presented by the choirs of the U.S. Naval Academy and Hood College in the U.S. Naval Academy Chapel. Tickets are free and can be obtained by writing Chapel Fund, Director of Musical Activities, Naval Academy, Annapolis, Maryland 21401. A performance of "The Nutcracker" is staged at St. John's College. An open house is a New Year's Day ritual at the Governor's Mansion and a Frost Bite Yacht Race takes place in the harbor.

To find out dates and more about holiday activities in Annapolis, call Historic Annapolis, Inc. at 301/267-8149.

Hunt Valley Inn

At Baltimore's Hunt Valley Inn a "Sip and Swap Party" is the innovative holiday celebration on Sunday following Christmas. Brunch features eggnog on the house. And here's your chance to do something with that Christmas gift you can't possibly use. Wrap, bring and exchange it for someone else's unusable present. The swap may not be your idea of the perfect gift, but you'll enjoy gourmet cuisine in the Cinnamon Tree Restaurant.

Cross Keys Inn

How about a "Golden Goose" for your Christmas dinner? Cross Keys Inn in Columbia, Maryland, serves a lavish buffet from noon until 10 pm. Serving venison is against the law in Maryland restaurants but every other conceivable holiday dish will adorn this sumptuous table. German bread pudding and French baba are among the vast assortment of desserts representing Christmas treats from around the world.

Bavarian Inn

Suckling pig is the main attraction for Christmas and New Year's dinner at the Bavarian Inn. Located in Shepherdstown, West Virginia, the Bavarian Inn celebrates the holidays with typical German food and decorations. Their large tree is decorated with old-fashioned wax candles, cookies, apples and unusual German ornaments.

In a greystone mansion on the banks of the Potomac, you can enjoy a different menu in a different kind of restaurant. Mrs. Hermione Golde pleased Washington diners for 20 years at the Bavarian Inn on 11th Street. You can still savor her potato dumplings and sweet-sour red cabbage with wiener schnitzel or wiener roast braten. For dessert it's a toss up between german chocolate cake, apple strudel or kuchen!

If John is your waiter, you are in for a floor show. One Saturday when everyone else had gone, he regaled us for an hour with fascinating stories of his fatherland. Also, with a little friendly persuasion, Mr. Golde might play some German folk songs for you in their attractive Rathskeller. Call 304/876-6070 for reservations.

There's no doubt about it, for two weeks, three days or one meal— Christmas is an Inn Season.

For more information or reservations, here are the numbers to call:
Boar's Head Inn, Williamsburg or Tides Inn 804/293-5350

Hunt Valley Inn 301/666-7000
Cross Keys Inn 301/730-3900
Bavarian Inn 304/876-6070

ELLICOTT CITY–TODAY'S YESTERDAY

Today's QUIET, WINDING MAIN STREET of Ellicott City was yesterday's highway to the West. Talking fast and not glancing outside the car, one might pass through Ellicott City and never know it. But this diminutive town in Maryland, with its unhurried pace, has a great deal of charm and is well worth a visit.

Old stone homes and stores dating back to the mid-1700's are niched into a rocky hillside. Turrets of a small castle can be seen high on a cliff overlooking the Patapsco Valley. Castle Angelo is a miniature copy of a French castle built in 1831. This quaint castle served as the original rectory for the first two Catholic priests of Ellicott City. The castle, also known as Angelo Cottage, harbors a ghost in its basement. Although it is not open to the public, the castle adds romance to the architectural skyline.

Perched atop another of Ellicott City's seven hills the county courthouse is encircled by fascinating small houses. These tiny structures housing law offices may have been inspired by the first Howard County Courthouse which is a tiny building measuring 12 by 18 feet. Viewing such small legal quarters prompted a friend to quip, "Justice seems to come in small packages in Howard County."

Land prices used to be about as small as the buildings. When Joseph, John and Andrew Ellicott, three Quaker brothers, founded this rural town and established their grist mill operation in 1772 they paid $3 an acre.

The most famous landmark in Ellicott City is the B&O Railroad Station at the foot of Main Street. Built in 1830, this rugged stone building was the first railroad depot in the United States. The old station was the scene of a race from Baltimore between a horse and "Tom Thumb," the first American-built locomotive. The horse won that particular race, but "Tom Thumb" and its successor won out as a significant means to increase Ellicott City's industrial importance. Today the station houses a railroad museum complete with a miniature model of the first 13 miles of B&O railroad track, a sight and sound show and gift shop. From the platform there is an excellent view of the mill, the hills, Tiber River and Main Street with its variety of intriguing shops.

This is a good place to park your car and start a leisurely walking tour. Many of the shops are filled with antiques, some are boutiques, others feature crafts and a few even sell essentials. Outside Paul's Market fruits and vegetables are right at your fingertips along with pens of live chickens and turkeys. (I'd almost forgotten that fowl came other than frozen.)

Ellicott's Country Store built in 1790 originally sold homemade candy and gingham bonnets. Its inventory has grown to include nearly anything you might be looking for. Mrs. Mildred Werner and her daughter are as happy to talk about the history of Ellicott City and the plans for restoring this historic area as they are to sell one of their imaginative pieces of doll furniture or dried flower sachets.

Being a clock fancier, I couldn't pass "Ye Old Town Watch and Clock Shoppe" without a peek in. What a vast and varied assortment! Although many of the timepieces were in for repair, Mr. Shaffer assured me over two hundred of the clocks were for sale. Two thousand seemed a more realistic figure to me. But whether you want to spend $2.00 or $2,000 you can find it here. Edgar Shaffer exudes the same enthusiasm that seems typical of these warm folks in Ellicott City. His was the second shop to open and he spoke with pride of his clocks and the newly acquired historic zoning for his town.

Old wearing apparel is a specialty at Edythe's Antiques and Boutique. Dresses and accessories from the Gay Nineties to the Roaring Twenties fill the racks. If you are looking for a costume for yourself or an antique dress for your teenage daughter, there are outfits to fill the bill.

Doll clothes and Christmas ornaments are featured at the Bird's Nest and I saw some handsome wood tables at The Fountainhead next door. Narrow steps in vault-like passages between some of the buildings lead to delightful patios and walled gardens. The Owl and Pussy Cat has a unique collection of handmade Christmas stockings. A black velvet and white lace stocking caught my eye, but I opted for a red calico with white ruffles.

The restaurant scene in Ellicott City is almost as varied as the shopping. Chez Fernand is a charming little French restaurant on the second floor of an old house. Sewing machine treadles are the pedestals for the tables. An unusual assortment of dark antique chairs enhance the red and white decor. Black wrought iron lanterns on the table and gas lamps on the walls add to Chez Fernand's pleasing ambience. Crepes are among the house specialties.

Cacao Lane is a French restaurant with a cave-like atmosphere—cool walls of old stone, brick floors and low ceilings. A bar and lounge are in one room, restaurant in another with tile tables and hanging baskets of greens.

For French-American cuisine in a country setting, you'll love Papillon. A gracious old home sits in the midst of 29 wooded acres. Old slave quarters have been converted into a pub. Random width floors and exposed beams add to its rustic appeal. Light meals are served here from 11 am 'til 1 am. Dinner is served in the elegant manor house. A charming verandah, sun room, formal dining rooms, private party rooms and a cozy cocktail lounge are all geared to your pleasure.

The most picturesque and most often photographed street in this quaint village is Tongue Row. A row of semi-detached granite houses curve around the side of a hill. Originally built as homes for mill-hands, these unique buildings now house art galleries and specialty shops. Behind the uneven roofline of Tongue Row can be glimpsed the soaring bell tower of the First Presbyterian Church. This architectural gem now serves as headquarters for the Howard County Historical Society.

Each season you'll discover a special attraction in Ellicott City. In August craftsmen dressed in old-fashioned costumes demonstrate their ancient methods of weaving, spinning and milling. Springtime finds the streets filled with flower markets and twice a year there is an outdoor art exhibit.

Christmas holidays are festive with something special planned for each weekend during December. Carollers stroll through the streets. Shops are gaily decorated, some serve hot cider and cookies. This is a great place to do your Christmas shopping. Far from the frustrations of crowded malls and city traffic, in an atmosphere reeking with nostalgia of the good old days.

Beltway Exit 23, Route 29N to Route 144. Turn right and you are there.

COLUMBIA –SPARKLING GEM OF MARYLAND

DESIGNED AND PLANNED AS A STEP toward solving the problems of our exploding cities, Columbia is gaining recognition as one of America's most successful new towns. Only 25 miles from Washington and 12 miles from Baltimore, Columbia, Maryland, is a sparkling man-made city.

Trees, lakes, parks, modern architecture and superb landscaping meld into a vibrant suburban-oriented community. Wide, shaded boulevards weave through a framework of neighborhood villages interspersed with recreational areas. "Downtown" is built on the edge of a beautiful lake.

In July 1967, Columbia's first residents moved into the Village of Wilde Lake. Today there are nearly 40,000 people living in six Columbia Villages. Its vast mall is one of the largest in the area with more than 100 shops and restaurants on two levels. The upper portion is carpeted while the lower area is paved with brick. Skylights bathe gardens, courtyards, pools and fountains with natural light, while attractive artificial lighting illumines the scene at night. Eventually, the Mall plans to include 300 stores. Personally, I prefer small individual shops, but it is entertaining to relax and watch the passing panorama in this perpetual springtime atmosphere.

Summer concerts at the Merriweather Post Pavillion have been popular since Columbia's very beginning. In fact, Symphony Woods, comprising 40 acres, was the first area to be developed in Columbia in 1966. Many young folks (and not so young) choose to picnic on the lawn while enjoying programs ranging from jazz to opera. Seating is also available in the covered Pavillion. Artists and special attractions are listed in the Washington and Baltimore papers.

Restaurants are continually being added to Columbia's dining scene. Clyde's serves great omelettes in a beautiful room overlooking the lake and presents live entertainment in the lounge. Entertainment is also a regular feature of Le Café, downtown, the Karrousel in Wilde Lake Village Green and the Hobbit's Glen Lounge at the golf course. In the Mall you have a choice of a Friendly Ice Cream Shop, a Chinese restaurant, a variety of snack bars and carry-out delis. At nearby King's Contrivance international cuisine is served in a 90-year old house with gracious Southern hospitality.

Cross Keys Inn serves excellent meals in a pleasant restaurant which has music and dancing in the evenings. You might enjoy a day or two at this handsome, modern Inn. Rooms are spacious and beautifully decorated. Some have saunas, others overlook a wooded stream.

There are two 18-hole golf courses in Columbia and a 36-hole miniature golf course called Fun-Putt. Indoor and outdoor tennis and swimming are available at several locations. Sailboats, rowboats, paddleboats and canoes can be rented from May through October on Kittamaqunde, the downtown lake. Skaters move in when the lake freezes over and from September through June an ice rink in Oakland Mills Village Center is whirling day and night.

The Columbia Horse Center, east on U.S. 29, offers equestrian instruction and horse shows throughout the year. There's also everything from rock to outdoor movies most summer nights at the lake-front plaza. The summer's festival is aimed at providing family-oriented fun free of charge. A twin movie theatre shows first-run films with no waiting in line or parking problems. For information on all Columbia programs and facilities call 301/730-6100.

Open plan teaching in the city's schools and openness of the community to people of varied backgrounds, ideas and aspirations are among Columbia's outstanding characteristics. Cooperative ministry by priests, rabbis and ministers in Columbia's Interfaith Center provides new vistas of understanding among congregations. New offices, industrial centers and research contribute to the area's economical development.

Although not scheduled for completion until the mid-1980's, Columbia is already a complete city, a complete playground and a complete getaway—a prosperous planned city in the midst of Maryland's countryside.

Directions: I-95 to Exit 23: North on Route 29.

SUGARLOAF MOUNTAIN –A SWEET CLIMB

WOULD YOU LIKE TO ESCAPE—NOT FROM—BUT *to* reality? Midway between Washington and Frederick, Sugarloaf Mountain looms on the horizon. So named because it reminded the early settlers of the sweet loaves popular in those days, Sugarloaf is today a singular area of peace and tranquility. Lacking the gaudy tourist trappings of most public parks, Sugarloaf is a special retreat for relaxation, enjoyment and an almost tangible spiritual uplift.

This was the ambition and desire of Gordon Strong. At the turn of the century, Mr. Strong bought the entire mountain, built his home and retired here at Sugarloaf. (So adamant was he against selling his mountain that he even refused Presidents Franklin D. Roosevelt and Harry S. Truman when they both tried to purchase the land for a retreat.) Instead, Gordon Strong willed his beloved mountain to the people to enjoy as though they were his personal guests. He further specified that Sugarloaf should be maintained in as natural a state as possible. So, from sun-up 'til sunset the trails and winding roads are open for hikers, bird watchers, botanists and nature lovers of all ages.

Viewing areas at different levels, facing in different directions, are spaced along a winding scenic drive. After climbing 415 steps to the very top of Sugarloaf (a signal station during the Civil War), you can usually see Washington Monument 30 miles in the distance.

A small gift shop with a rustic atmosphere sells antiques, paintings and handicrafts by local artists. A refreshment stand sells light snacks and

173

throughout the woods picnic tables are provided for family groups. But for a hearty meal and panoramic view of Sugarloaf, Comus Inn is nearby.

A spacious country home turned into a restaurant, this rambling Inn has many rooms including a sundeck across the back with large windows framing the mushroom-like mountain. Soups and desserts are homemade. A nearby barn has been converted into a fascinating antique shop.

While abiding by the stipulations of Mr. Strong's will, Stronghold, Inc. is able to preserve this natural landmark while making progressive strides in the ecological climate at the same time. Great plans are underway for a laboratory or experimental station to work toward eradicating the dreaded chestnut blight. Also in the making is a small plant nursery, a wildflower garden and a nature center.

Shakespeare said, "One touch of nature makes the whole world kin." Emerson said, "In the woods is perpetual youth." Centuries and continents apart, Shakespeare, Emerson and Strong shared a common bond. In Gordon Strong's own words, "When one stands on the summit of the mountain, the sheer cliff hanging over the wild and wooded slopes below, looking out over the peaceful and lovely Frederick Valley, looking at the Catoctin and Blue Ridge rising to meet the lowering sun, for a moment at least one experiences an inspiration, a moral uplift."

And so Sugarloaf Mountain, untrammeled and unspoiled, provides the perfect escape—not from—but *to* reality.

Directions: I-95 to Exit 17 or 18 to 270. 22 miles to Route 109; turn left, 3 miles to Comus; turn right, 2 miles to Sugarloaf.

FRAMED BY THE MAJESTIC BAY BRIDGE, in the shadows of the famed U.S. Naval Academy, Annapolis is a natural watercolor beyond compare. Few small towns combine so beautifully the rich heritage of our past with the vibrancy of today's living.

Annapolis has been described as a living museum embracing three centuries of architectural development—one of the few places where American master-pieces of art and architecture may be seen in their original setting. Its lovely old Georgian homes have been lived in continuously since they were built, and the State House is the nation's oldest capitol still in legislative use.

Two circles dominate the historic seaport town: Church Circle with its towering spire and State Circle with the great white dome of the Capitol. Here you can view the oldest U.S. flag in existence or visit the senate chamber where George Washington resigned his commission and where the Treaty of Paris was signed in 1784.

Radiating from these circles are quaint and picturesque streets. Some are cobblestone with tiny "ship-lap" houses; a few are narrow brick-paved lanes with alluring antique and specialty shops; others are tree-lined with gracious dwellings.

A unique warmth permeates Annapolis. You sense it as you walk through the restored buildings, as you stroll along pretty streets and particularly when you reach the City Dock. A present-day yachting center, this scenic dock area was a seaport which won fame during the Colonial, Revolutionary and Federal days. Its jewel-like harbor is still busy. There are boats of every description—spectacular sailboats, sleek white yachts, rugged working boats, even remnants of the only commercial skipjack fleet still operating in America.

The old City Market with produce stands and raw bars is a colorful part of the City Dock. This is the scene also of the Maryland Clam Festival the first weekend in August and the Annapolis Fine Arts Festival on the third weekend in June. The Summer Garden Theatre is nearby as well as old taverns and seafood restaurants.

Although Annapolis has heard but faintly the quiet sounds of change, there is a flourishing number of excellent restaurants adding to the original seafood scene—Italian, French and Continental.

Middleton Tavern on the City Dock has been a favorite with Annapolites for a century or so. Crepes filled with everything from strawberries to caviar are yummy at La Crepe Normandy on Main Street. Soup and sandwich is the featured lunch at The Barrister Inn. A huge antique library serves as the unique backbar at this attractive old restaurant across from the Capitol.

For brunch with the flavor of New Orleans, go to the Maryland Inn. In their intimate Treaty of Paris Restaurant you can order eye-openers like champagne and eggs benedict or bloody marys and crab omelettes.

This venerable old Inn was built during the Revolution on the prominant lot laid out for the use of the town's drummer. Although its rooms have been up-dated with modern comforts, they are individually decorated to preserve the period charm. Fine walnut bannisters, decorative original woodwork and many of the fireplaces have been intact. Legislators attending the Maryland General Assembly and visitors to the Naval Academy enjoy the superb location of this wedge shape hotel. Charlie Byrd uses its subterranean King of France Tavern as headquarters for his famed guitar concerts.

The Annapolis Hilton has a real vantage point on the harbor. The Penthouse Restaurant and some of its rooms have balconies overlooking the Bay. Others look out over the roof tops and chimneys of this captivating town, which boasts many varieties of architectural styles. Still others face the United States Naval Academy.

Founded in 1845, the Academy comprises 300 acres with modern buildings complementing the original French Renaissance style. Midshipmen numbering 4,200 and a faculty of 600 continue to meet the challenge of combining military and spiritual strength.

The Naval Chapel, epitomizing this spirit, has been referred to as "the most important shrine of American naval tradition—a building of harmony, magnitude, elegance and lofty dignity." Each cherished detail has a significant meaning, and a visit to this sacred cathedral proves an enriching experience. Its doors are open to the public every day, including Sunday Church services (Catholic, 9 am, Protestant, 11 am) and on the fourth Sunday of each month you can enjoy a recital of organ music.

The chapel is a treasure-house of gifts and memorials with the crypt of John Paul Jones, father of the American Navy located beneath the chancel. Visitors are also welcome to tour the museum, which contains the finest collection of naval memorabilia in the country and a world-famous collection of ship models.

The entire downtown section of Annapolis (one square mile) is designated a Registered National Historic District. Historic Annapolis, Inc. keeps its benevolent eye on the town from a tiny building on the Capitol lawn. Originally the Treasury, this petite house is the oldest public building in America. Volunteers with this non-profit organization are knowledgeable about the history and pleasures in Annapolis. Taking great pride in their legendary town, they are exceptionally friendly and helpful.

Whether you take a guided walking tour or go on your own, you will sense the influence of religion, education, government, commerce and culture.

Handsome homes of three signers of the Declaration of Independence are open to the public. William Paca's House with terraced Italian gardens has been recently restored. Located on Prince Street right off Maryland Avenue, it will eventually serve as a guest house for foreign dignitaries invited to the United States by the State Department. Hammond Harwood's fine house is regarded as one of the most perfect examples of Georgian architecture anywhere. Thomas Jefferson adopted some of the harmonious innovations of this house for his home in Monticello. Another home on Maryland Avenue achieved historical significance when Francis Scott Key, composer of the "Star Spangled Banner" was married at the Chase-Lloyd House. Baroque features here include ornately carved woodwork and silver keyholes.

Many old homes along Maryland Avenue have been converted into shops and restaurants. Often referred to as "Old Timer's Main Street" and "Antique Row," this is one of the most delightful streets in town to browse.

You'll also enjoy a walk around the campus of St. John's College. Chartered in 1784 as the first college to prohibit religious discrimination, it embraces almost all American history. Francis Scott Key graduated in 1796. During the Civil War it was utilized as a hospital. Coeducational since 1951, St. John's offers a unique curriculum which seeks to teach men and women how to think. The Liberty Tree, one of Maryland's most historic trees and estimated to be more than 600 years old, is the scene of graduation ceremonies each spring.

I don't believe there's a spot in town where history or local color isn't in evidence. Rumor has it George Washington had his hair cut in the barber shop at

No. 6 Cornhill Street. You can catch glimpses of the hardy men who go dredging for oysters in winter months around an old pot-bellied stove at Sadler's Fish Market (310 3rd Street, across Eastport Bridge). In fact, the winter bay is as exciting as the summer sea—white sails looming as dramatically against skies of grey as those of blue.

To an old area saying, "Walk a mile, stay a week," I enthusiastically add: "And return frequently" to Annapolis—a town for all seasons.

Directions: I-95 to Exit 30, Route 50.

Index

183

184